LAW™

Personal Legal Sourcebooks

. . . .

Incorporation

. . . .

MACMILLAN SPECTRUM

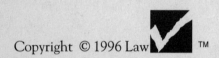
International Standard Book Number: 0-02-861402-X
Library of Congress Card Catalog Number: 96-068548

98 97 96   9 8 7 6 5 4 3 2 1

Interpretation of the printing code: the rightmost number of the first series of numbers is the year of the book's printing; the rightmost number of the second series of numbers is the number of the book's printing. For example, a printing code of 96-1 shows that the first printing occurred in 1996.

Printed in the United States of America

Note: Reasonable care has been taken in the preparation of the text to ensure its clarity and accuracy. This book is sold with the understanding that the author and the publisher are not engaged in rendering legal, accounting, or other professional service. Laws vary from state to state, and readers with specific financial questions should seek the services of a professional advisor.

The author and publisher specifically disclaim any liability, loss, or risk, personal or otherwise, which is incurred as a consequence, directly or indirectly, of the use and application of any of the contents of this book.

Book Design by A&D Howell.

Contents

Preface

Welcome to the layman's guide to corporations. The purpose of this book is to provide the general public some information about corporations. It is a reference manual that should answer basic questions. The questions recited in this manual are the more commonly asked questions of attorneys when a client first makes contact for the purpose of forming a new company. Neither this manual nor the subject matter contained within is in any way a substitute for legal advice. For legal advice, an attorney must be consulted.

The design of this manual is elementary and is, by no means, a comprehensive assessment of a particular legal discipline. It will, however, allow the reader to better understand the various aspects of corporations.

Hopefully, the use of this manual will lessen the personal agony of attempting to look up the answers to the questions covered here. Additionally, the manual should reduce the amount of time the reader will ultimately spend with chosen legal counsel and, therefore, reduce to some degree the costs of legal services.

On the other hand, the manual is also designed to bring to the legal community a better educated public. The massive amount of legal information that is available to the individual attorney would, without question, overwhelm a member of the public who is not trained to research and retrieve the information that would typically apply to a given subject such as corporations. A competent attorney who is skilled in providing legal advice relative to corporation law should welcome a client with a basic understanding of how a corporation is operated. Therefore, the reader should take comfort in the fact that through the choice of this manual, it will be possible to meet in the attorney's office with a greater understanding of the subject matter involved.

This manual gives an overview and basic understanding through a question-and-answer format. It also furnishes some basic forms that most likely would be used in a given state. This manual should provide the general types of forms that an attorney might employ in preparing and filing the necessary documents for incorporation.

It is never recommended that an individual undertake his or her own representation in such matters as corporations, even though most states do permit such activity. Any individual who is serious about forming a proper corporation would want to have capable legal assistance. In that regard, the reader is urged to contact a competent attorney who, as mentioned above, should welcome the fact that a client is arriving at his or her office with the information acquired from this manual. In other words, the reader should be a better informed member of the public by reading and reviewing the contents of this manual and, accordingly, should be better prepared to consult an attorney about a new corporation.

Read on, and enjoy the world of corporations!

Introduction

Nearly every American who is not an attorney has, at one time or another, wondered about the legal profession and what it would be like to acquire at least a portion of the knowledge seemingly guarded by the legal community. Many times the average individual has the misconception that attorneys safeguard this information for their own benefit and for the sole purpose of protecting their livelihood. That is not the reason the legal information has not been disseminated to the public. Frankly, no one has undertaken the effort until this time to prepare a system of manuals that would introduce the public to some of the basic information on individual subject areas of the law.

It is not a conspiracy by the legal community to keep information from the general public. It is not because of the unique legal training received by attorneys that information is not readily available to the public. It is not because of the special features of legal language that the information about the law is not found in general reference. The bottom line is simply that there is so very much information written in each state about the laws of that state. In addition, federal laws often apply, and the federal ramifications must be taken into consideration.

Consequently, the body of law that relates to a given area, or as we call it in this publication "discipline" of the law, is so immense that even the most skilled attorney in a particular field, such as corporate law, would have no way of memorizing or remembering all of the applicable law for his field of study in a single state. The training that an individual attorney receives allows him or her to readily find the necessary material and properly and skillfully represent the client. Of course, we're speaking of competent attorneys, and the public should understand that the majority of attorneys fall into that category.

The vast body of law that is available to attorneys is often available to the general public either through a public library in some instances or through a law library generally situated at the location of a law school, a major university or a major corporation. Many times the librarians of those facilities will permit members of the public to browse through the legal information that is also available to attorneys. However, without appropriate training, those attempting to ascertain answers to even simple questions may find themselves spending endless hours or days on a particular subject. They may also end up misleading themselves if they allow their research to take them in a wrong direction. Therefore, despite what many people believe, there is a vital need for the legal community and competent legal advice. On the other hand, there is an equally vital need for the public to have access to understandable legal reference material in order to be better informed when contacting their attorney.

The Law™ Manual and Presentation

Since there has been so much confusion regarding any particular subject area of the law, and since that confusion seems to increase due to the limited reporting of various legal matters by the media, an eminent need exists for the general public to have at their fingertips some basic information about the law and particular legal subjects. In an effort to bring the general public up to speed, Lawchek undertook the publication of various manuals on various topics of the law in order to bring some of the basic information to the general public in readable form. In turn, it is the expectation of Lawchek that the public will be better informed when conferring with a member of the legal community on a given subject of the law. The Lawchek philosophy was to break the legal material down by subject matter.

Throughout the publications provided by Lawchek, the consumer will observe that even though the general topics are broken down by state, there are numerous instances where federal law might be significant and apply to a given question. In those cases, a synopsis of the federal law has been provided so that the member of the public can, in turn, inquire of his or her legal counsel appropriately. The general public also needed to be guided through a system by which the topics of general concern could be identified and explained. Consequently, Lawchek divided the subject matter not only by state but by "discipline."

Disciplines of the Law

The disciplines, or topics of the law, which have been chosen by Lawchek are the disciplines which Lawchek surveys indicate to be matters of most common interest. There are literally thousands of topics for research under the general body of law and hundreds of those topics break down even further into subtopics. Many of the topics and subtopics can be interrelated and essentially cross the paths of other topics depending upon a factual scenario which may develop in a given situation. For example, a corporation may have a contract with an individual and that contract, in turn, may be involved with financing through a particular bank which, in turn, may require certain collateral and a specific form of insurance. In this scenario, it is understandable that corporation law, contract law, the uniform commercial code, banking law, and insurance law might all apply, to name the most obvious. In a more specific area from the same scenario, it might be necessary for an appropriate application for a secured transaction to fall under the uniform commercial code and, in such cases, a particular form for filing with either a secretary of state or the local county recorder may come into the picture. It can be seen from this simple example that the various topics or disciplines of the law are so interrelated that an effort by your attorney to research the particulars under any one of those topics may be necessary.

It is not the purpose of the Lawchek information or reference manual, which you now have in your hand, to deal with any in-depth legal issues which would obviously involve the research of a competent attorney. This manual is exclusively designed to enable you to have an overview of the discipline (in this case corporations) before you consult with your attorney and/or before you decide whether you do or do not feel you should incorporate. The structure by Lawchek into the discipline method of reference explanations for the public is also provided to give the public an appreciation of the type of format that is used in presenting a legal document to an appropriate authority. An example of this would be the articles of incorporation that may be presented to the secretary of state for filing. By having an awareness of the forms as well as an awareness of the basic information about the discipline, you should be far better equipped to consult your attorney about incorporating.

Lawchek has identified thirty disciplines which either are now available or will soon be available through either Macmillan General Reference or Macmillan Library Reference.

- Administrative Law
- Agricultural Law
- Banking
- Bankruptcy
- Business/Commercial Law
- Contracts
- Criminal
- Corporations
- Domestic/Family Law
- Education
- Eminent Domain/Condemnation
- Elderly
- Environment
- Estates and Wills
- Health
- Insurance

- Intellectual Property (Patent/Copyright)
- International Law (Nafta/Trade)
- Interstate Commerce
- Investments/Brokerage
- Landlord/Tenant
- Manufacturing
- Media (TV-Common Radio, Newspaper)
- Partnerships
- Real Estate
- Social Security
- Sports Law
- Taxation
- Transportation
- Trials/Litigation
- Truth in Lending

Is a Little Knowledge Dangerous?

There is no doubt that a little knowledge in the wrong hands may be dangerous, especially if that knowledge is misused or misinterpreted. That is why Lawchek recommends that the reader contact a competent attorney before undertaking the task of incorporating. Presently, the public has far too little knowledge at its fingertips about the law and the legal community. This lack of knowledge has created many misconceptions about corporate law. The design and purpose of this manual is to increase your knowledge and bring you to a better understanding of the subject matter of corporations.

The information contained in this booklet is basic, practical information. The manual is designed to bring to you some knowledge about the subject matter of corporations. Lawchek wants the general public to be better informed about the law and recognizes, as Lawchek is certain the reader does, that if you're going to do something—do it right. This manual is designed to take you to that first step so that you have a basic understanding of corporations before you confer with an attorney. This will enable you to make a better choice as to which attorney you might select to represent you in your new corporation. This manual will place you in a better position when it comes to understanding the legal work involved in forming your new corporation. Remember, you do want your new corporation to be organized properly and you want to have an understanding of what is being done. This manual will help you with a better understanding of the legal processes. Selecting a competent attorney who understands incorporating is part of doing it right.

How to Use This Book

This book is divided into five sections:

Chapter 1—Definition of Terms. Various terms that are used throughout this book are defined in Part 1. These definitions will assist you with the legal language used throughout and give you a better idea about corporations in general.

Chapter 2—Do's and Don'ts. Chapter 2 deals with major pitfalls that can occur and the fact that there are certain things you will want to do and certain things you will not want to do in setting up your new corporation. At any time where there is doubt, you should consult your attorney.

Chapter 3—Questions and Answers. A question and answer format is set forth in Chapter 3. These are the questions most commonly asked about incorporating. The answers to these questions may relate specifically to your state.

Chapter 4—Sample Forms. Generally, the forms are tailored for a particular state. In this manual, they are generic and must be modified for particular state use. These forms are current to the date of this publication. If legislative enactments have occurred since the publication date, the forms may need to be changed accordingly. This is why it is important to consult your attorney.

Chapter 5—Blank Forms. The forms in this chapter are blank versions of the completed forms in Chapter 4; these forms are for your use.

The recommended practice for the use of this manual is for you to find the question that concerns you in the question-and-answer portion, then find the form that applies in the form section. We recommend that you first read the section on common terms. By cross-referencing between the questions and answers and the appropriate forms, you will see that it is much easier to understand the forms and much easier to prepare them for your attorney.

Because the information provided by Lawchek may not be all-inclusive to corporate law, you are advised that any questions you have that go beyond the questions and answers or forms provided in this manual, should be presented to your attorney. Although the material contained in all of Lawchek's manuals has been written by attorneys, these attorneys are located throughout the United States and focus their study of law in particular areas. It would both be improper and unethical for Lawchek to serve as a clearinghouse in referring you to those attorneys. Therefore, Lawchek cannot and will not make such references but encourages you to contact your own attorney with skills in the area of corporations. Should you need assistance in locating such an attorney, you should contact the Bar Association for a listing of names of attorneys in your state who do practice in the area of corporations.

Codes, Sections, and Subsections

Throughout the Lawchek program, references are made to legal codes, sections, and subsections (§). Examples of these references are Massachusetts Code 231:85P, Section 3109.01 of the Ohio

Revised Code, §4-27-301 of the Arkansas Code. Should the reader choose to research this legal information on their own, the information may be accessed at the law library of a major college or university. However, it should be noted that law libraries are not organized in the same manner as other libraries. Anyone attempting to undertake his or her own research should be prepared to confront a difficult, tedious task. It is very advisable that an attorney or someone else familiar with legal research be consulted.

Acknowledgments

Many people contributed in various ways toward making this legal reference material available to the general public, and it would be impossible to acknowledge them all. However, special thanks must be given to several people who were indispensable to the completion of this manual.

For his countless hours of legal research and his ability to interpret that research into text that is understandable to those not having a legal background, Lawchek would like to thank Attorney Richard A. Pundt.

Lawchek is indebted to Debra A. Shiley and Bette Tropek Miller for their time and diligence in transcribing, proofreading, and editing the booklet and assuring the quality of the final product.

Trademarks/Copyrights

All material of Lawchek is protected with appropriate trademarks and copyrights. Additionally, terms mentioned in this book that are known to be or suspected to be the trademarks or service marks of other companies are capitalized and such terms and conditions are also capitalized or highlighted or specially acknowledged in the software that may accompany this manual. Lawchek cannot attest to the accuracy of this information. The use of a term in this book should not be regarded as affecting the validity of any trademark or service mark.

Definition of Terms

The following list of definitions will assist you with the legal language used throughout the book and give you a better idea about incorporation law in general.

Aggregate stock—The aggregate stock is the total amount of stock that a corporation is authorized to issue through its articles or charter or certificate of incorporation.

Asset—An asset is generally a form of property. It may be real or personal, and it may include tangibles or intangibles. It may even be patents or copyrights that are owned by an individual or a corporation.

Board of directors—The board of directors is made up of the individuals who operate a corporation and to whom the officers of a corporation must answer. The board of directors generally sets the policy and direction of a corporation and its operations.

Bylaws—Bylaws of a corporation are the rules by which the shareholders run the corporation.

Capitalization—Capitalization is the sum of money used to create the financial existence of an entity such as a corporation.

Commerce—Commerce is usually the exchange of goods, productions, or property of any kind where buying or selling is involved.

Committee—A committee is generally a group of persons who have assembled for a designated or specific purpose. In most cases, a committee is set up to perform a specific task on behalf of the entity, such as a corporation, which charges the committee with that task.

Contract—A contract is an agreement between two or more persons, including a corporation, that creates an obligation to do or not to do a particular thing.

Corporate book—The corporate book generally contains the official documents of the corporation.

Corporate entity—A corporate entity is the distinct or unique status of a corporation that sets it apart and its existence apart from that of its individual shareholders.

Corporate name—The corporate name is the name that a corporation uses to conduct business. Generally, the corporation's name must include certain specific requirements according to each state's laws. Those requirements may include the abbreviation Inc., Co., Corp., and/or Ltd.

Corporate officers—The corporate officers of a company are the people who fill the offices of the company and who conduct the business for the day-to-day operations. Officers may include the president, vice president, secretary, and treasurer.

Corporation—The corporation is an artificial entity created by state law. It is usually an association of persons who are brought together to form the entity for a specific investment or other purpose. Under the law, a corporation is treated as an individual and may sue or be sued. A corporation is distinct from the individuals who own its shares. A corporation also survives in the event of the death of an individual shareholder.

Expense—An expense is generally that which is an outlay, charge, cost, or price of something. An expenditure of time, money, or effort may be construed to be an expense.

Incorporate—To incorporate means to create or set up a corporation.

Incorporation—Incorporation is generally the act or process of forming a corporation. It is the act of making a corporation a legal entity.

Investment—An investment is generally an expenditure made to acquire property or another asset generally for the purpose of producing revenue. Generally, it is the placing of capital in a way intended to secure income from profit gained by the use of that capital.

Joint venture—A joint venture is usually an undertaking by more than one individual or corporation for mutual benefit or mutual profit. Most generally it is where individuals contribute certain assets and share certain risks.

Lawful—Lawful means something that is legal or authorized by the law. Specific statutes may qualify what a party or corporation may or may not do under the law.

Legal age—Legal age generally means the age at which a person acquires the capacity to make and enter into his or her own contracts. This age may vary from state to state.

Legal entity—Legal entity generally means legal existence; an entity other than a natural person that has an existence recognized by the law, such as a corporation.

Liability—Liability is a very broad term but, generally, means a responsibility or obligation that arises out of the occurrence of some hazard or act. It also relates to debts and obligations.

Lien—A claim, encumbrance, or charge on the property for payment of some debt, obligation, or duty.

Meeting minutes—The meeting minutes of a corporation are generally a printed recounting of the actions taken by the board of directors or the shareholders of a corporation.

Meetings—In a corporate sense, meetings mean the calling together of either the board of directors or the shareholders or both for the purpose of carrying out the official acts of the corporation.

Organization—Organization usually means to place together or bring together the elements necessary for forming a corporation. It is generally where two or more people have a common interest to place in operation through a series of steps an entity such as a company.

President—The president of a corporation is generally in charge of a company's operations. The duties and obligations of the president may be regulated by the bylaws of the company.

Property—Property is generally an item that has an ownership quality. It is an item that belongs to an individual or a corporation. It generally has a determined amount of value and usually denotes anything that is the subject of ownership (tangible or intangible).

Purpose—The purpose for a corporation is usually defined in the articles of incorporation. The corporation purpose may also be subject to certain state laws. It sets out the reason for the corporation's existence.

Ratification of acts—Ratification generally means the confirmation and acceptance of certain acts that are undertaken on behalf of an entity such as a corporation.

Real estate—Real estate is generally understood to be land or anything permanently affixed to the land, such as buildings, fences, etc. Real estate is generally synonymous with real property or realty.

Registered agent—A registered agent is a natural person or a corporation authorized to act on behalf of a corporation, such as accepting service of process in the event the corporation is sued. It is the person who would be contacted relative to official business of the corporation.

Registered office—A registered office is the location of a particular company. It is generally the official office where service of process may be made upon a company and is also the office where the official documents including minutes are maintained.

Secretary—The secretary of a corporation is generally the individual who maintains the books and records of the corporation. The secretary also reads and approves the various minutes, stock certificates that are issued, and any other official documents that are issued by the corporation. Most generally, the president and the secretary need to sign documents evidencing ownership or claims against ownership such as stocks, bonds, or debentures. However, it is usually the secretary alone who signs the corporate minutes and keeps the minutes of the company.

Secretary of state—The secretary of state is the official, usually elected by the general public, who manages the business affairs of a given state. Generally, it is the secretary of state who collects the fees for state operations, including filing fees of corporations. In some states, it may be a specific officer other than the secretary of state who registers corporations.

Stock—The stock for a corporation includes any equity, securities, or instruments that are issued by the corporation. This is exclusive of any bonds or debentures. Bonds or debentures usually reflect debt rather than stock or equity ownership. Stock is generally evidenced by some written document that demonstrates the ownership in a corporation. It generally identifies the company, the name of the stockholder, the class and/or series, and, many times, the value of the stock.

Stock certificate—A stock certificate is the document that evidences stock ownership in a corporation. A stock certificate will generally indicate the state in which the certificate has been issued, the date of issue, the amount of par value, and the number of shares that the certificate represents. It denotes ownership in a company and is evidence of that ownership. Generally, it is signed and dated by the president and secretary of the corporation.

Trade name—A trade name is the name that may be used by a company to identify the company business. Many times the trade name epitomizes the reputation of the business.

Transaction—A transaction is an act of conducting business between a corporation or persons for which generally there is some form of documentation.

Treasurer—A treasurer of a corporation is the individual who maintains the books of account and financial records of the corporation. The treasurer is generally in charge of making appropriate deposits and seeing that withdrawals are made according to the company resolutions and/or bank resolutions.

Treasury stock—Treasury stock is generally stock that had been issued as fully paid to stockholders and, subsequently, reacquired by the corporation.

Vice president—The vice president most generally acts in the absence of the president; however, there may be special duties or functions set forth in the bylaws relative to the specific circumstances under which a vice president must act.

Do's and Don'ts

Do

Read this manual.

Remember to consult an attorney for legal problems.

Read Chapter 3, "Questions and Answers," in order to have a basic understanding of the subject matter that you have chosen, in this case, corporations.

Pay special attention to detail, especially when completing forms for your attorney.

Approach incorporation as a serious matter that requires patience for the long term and guidance to complete.

Enjoy the materials presented and use the materials for your benefit in acquiring new knowledge.

Don't

Make assumptions about corporate law.

Expect this manual to be the substitute or a replacement for an attorney's implementation of incorporating procedures.

Expect that the questions and answers embellish all aspects of incorporating.

Expect the forms contained here to be the only forms that you may need.

Rush through the materials or make assumptions Consult an attorney.

Expect that just anyone will have the answers to your questions. Read the manual and talk to your attorney.

Questions and Answers

The questions below are the most commonly asked about incorporating. The answers relate specifically to each state.

What is a corporation?

A corporation, according to *Black's Law Dictionary*, is an artificial person or legal entity created by or under the authority of the laws of a state. It is an association of persons created by statute as a legal entity. The law treats the corporation itself as a person who can sue and be sued. The corporation is distinct from the individuals (shareholders) who comprise it. The corporation survives the death of its investors, as the shares can usually be transferred. The corporate entity subsists as a political body under a special domination, which is regarded in law as having a personality and existence distinct from that of its several members. By the same authority, it is vested with the capacity of continuous succession, irrespective of changes in its membership, either in perpetuity or for a limited term of years. It acts as a unit or single individual in matters relating to the common purpose of the association, within the scope of the powers and authorities conferred upon the corporation by law.

What does corporate existence mean?

Unless a delayed effective date is specified within the articles, the corporate existence begins when the articles of incorporation are filed with the secretary of state.

Who are incorporators?

Alabama: Incorporators may be individuals of legal age.

Alaska: One or more natural persons, at least eighteen years of age, may act as an incorporator of a corporation by signing, verifying, and delivering to the commissioner an original and exact copy of the articles of incorporation. When reference is made to the commissioner, such reference is the Commissioner of Commerce and Economic Development in the state of Alaska.

Arizona: A person who acts as an incorporator in the state of Arizona must deliver the articles of incorporation to the state's corporation commission for filing.

Arkansas: One or more natural persons, at least eighteen years of age, may act as an incorporator or incorporators of a corporation by signing, verifying, and delivering the articles of incorporation to the secretary of state for filing.

California: One or more natural persons, partnerships, associations, or corporations, domestic or foreign, may form a corporation under Division 1 of Title 1 of the California Corporation Code by executing and filing the articles of incorporation with the secretary of state. If directors are named, the individual directors must sign and acknowledge the articles. If directors have not been named, then the articles must be signed by the individuals acting as incorporators.

Colorado: One or more natural persons may act as an incorporator of a corporation by signing, verifying, and delivering in duplicate to the secretary of state, the articles of incorporation for the company.

Connecticut: One or more individuals may be incorporators as provided by Section 33-285. The incorporators must appoint a statutory agent for services all in conjunction with Section 33-296.

Delaware: Any person of legal age may act as an incorporator under the laws of Delaware. In Delaware any person, partnership, association, or corporation without regard to residence, domicile, or state of incorporation may incorporate or organize an organization by filing with the Division of Corporations in the Department of State a certificate of incorporation executed pursuant to Section 103 of the General Corporation Law.

Florida: Any person of legal age may incorporate in the state of Florida.

Georgia: One or more persons may act as the incorporator or incorporators for a corporation in Georgia by delivering the articles of incorporation to the secretary of state for filing.

Hawaii: Any individual intending to organize a corporation or individuals who are officers of the corporation or a majority of the incorporators or any person or persons as the court may designate may act as an incorporator under the laws of Hawaii.

Idaho: Any person may act as an incorporator in the state of Idaho. The incorporators must deliver the articles of incorporation to the secretary of state for filing.

Illinois: In Illinois, one or more incorporators (signers of the original articles of incorporation) may organize a company under the Illinois Business Corporation Act of 1983. An incorporator may be a person over the age of eighteen or a corporation (domestic or foreign).

Indiana: Any person may act as an incorporator under the laws of the state of Indiana.

Iowa: An incorporator is a person who acts as an incorporator in the state of Iowa and must deliver the articles of incorporation to the secretary of state for filing.

Kansas: Any person of legal age may act as an incorporator in the state of Kansas. Other entities may also incorporate in the state of Kansas.

Kentucky: One or more persons may act as an incorporator by delivering articles of incorporation to the secretary of state for filing.

Louisiana: One or more natural or artificial persons capable of contracting may incorporate in the state of Louisiana.

Maine: One or more natural persons, domestic corporations, or foreign corporations may incorporate in the state of Maine. It is not necessary for that individual corporator to be a resident of the state of Maine. Each domestic corporation must have, and maintain in the state, a clerk who is a natural person of the state. The clerk shall maintain a registered office. The contents of the corporate name are regulated under Section 301.

Maryland: To properly form a corporation in Maryland, one or more adult individuals must sign and acknowledge articles of incorporation and shall file the articles with the department.

Massachusetts: In the commonwealth of Massachusetts, the incorporators must associate themselves with the intention of forming a corporation and must so state. Once they have formed together for the purpose of preparing the articles of organization, they must be certain that same are filed in conjunction with Chapter 156B.

Michigan: One or more persons must file articles of incorporation with the administrator in the state of Michigan, under Section 21.200(131).

Minnesota: One or more natural persons of full age may act as incorporators by filing articles of incorporation with the secretary of state.

Mississippi: One or more persons may act as the incorporator or incorporators of a corporation by delivering articles of incorporation to the secretary of state.

Missouri: One or more individuals of the age of eighteen or older may be incorporators by signing, verifying, and delivering the articles of incorporation in duplicate to the office of the secretary of state.

Montana: One or more natural persons, at least eighteen years of age, may incorporate in the state of Montana.

Nebraska: One or more natural persons, at least eighteen years of age, may act as an incorporator or incorporators of a corporation by signing, verifying, and delivering the articles of incorporation to the secretary of state for filing.

Nevada: One or more natural persons may associate with each other to form a corporation for the transaction of any lawful business or to promote or to conduct any legitimate object or purpose, pursuant to and subject to Chapter 78 of the Nevada Revised Statutes.

New Hampshire: A corporation in New Hampshire may be organized by three or fewer co-owners, by corporation, partnership, trust, estate, or other entity. It may be operated by trustees, guardians, custodians, or other fiduciaries.

New Jersey: One or more individuals, at least eighteen years or older, or domestic or foreign corporations may act as incorporators. The incorporators need not be United States citizens or residents of New Jersey, nor do they need to be subscribers to shares in the corporation.

New Mexico: One or more natural persons of legal age may act as an incorporator of a corporation.

New York: One or more natural persons, at least eighteen years of age, may act as an incorporator or incorporators of a corporation in the state of New York and must deliver the certificate of incorporation to the secretary of state for filing.

North Carolina: One or more natural persons, at least eighteen years of age, may act as an incorporator or incorporators in the state of North Carolina.

North Dakota: Anyone of legal age may be an incorporator in the state of North Dakota.

Ohio: Any person, singly or jointly, with others and without regard to residence, domicile, or state of incorporation, may form a corporation by signing and filing the articles of incorporation with the secretary of state.

Oklahoma: Any person, partnership, association, or corporation, singly or jointly with others, and without regard to their residence, domicile, or state of incorporation, may incorporate or organize a corporation pursuant to the provisions of the Oklahoma General Corporation Act by filing a certificate of incorporation with the secretary of state.

Oregon: One or more natural persons, at least eighteen years of age, may act as an incorporator or incorporators of a corporation.

Pennsylvania: One or more corporations or natural persons of full age may incorporate a business corporation in the state of Pennsylvania.

Rhode Island: One or more persons of legal age may be incorporators in the state of Rhode Island. Any person of legal age may begin a corporation by delivering duplicate articles of incorporation to the secretary of state for filing.

South Carolina: Any person may act as an incorporator under the laws of South Carolina. He or she must deliver the articles of incorporation to the secretary of state for filing pursuant to Section 33-2-101.

South Dakota: One or more natural persons, at least eighteen years of age, may act as an incorporator or incorporators of a corporation by signing, verifying, and delivering the articles of incorporation to the secretary of state for filing.

Tennessee: Any person, singly or jointly with others, and without regard to residence, domicile, or state of incorporation, may form a corporation by signing and filing the articles of incorporation with the secretary of state.

Texas: An incorporator may be any natural person of the age of eighteen or a partnership, a corporation, an association, a trust, or an estate.

Utah: Three or more natural persons, eighteen years or older, may act as incorporators of a corporation by signing, verifying, and delivering an original and one copy of the articles of incorporation for the corporation to the Division of Corporations and Commercial Code.

Vermont: In Vermont, one or more natural persons of the age of majority may act as incorporators by delivering the articles of incorporation in duplicate to the secretary of state for filing.

Virginia: Incorporators in the commonwealth of Virginia may be one or more persons who sign and file articles of incorporation with the commission. The incorporators must file articles of incorporation with the commission for approval, providing the appropriate fees with the forms prescribed for articles of incorporation.

Washington: In the state of Washington, one or more persons may incorporate or act as incorporators by filing the articles of incorporation with the secretary of state.

West Virginia: One or more persons, or a domestic or foreign corporation may act as an incorporator or incorporators of a corporation by signing and delivering the articles of incorporation in duplicate to the secretary of state. (See Section 31-1-26.)

Wisconsin: Under Wisconsin law, one or more persons may act as the incorporator or incorporators of a corporation. Following the incorporation of a corporation, a majority of the incorporators or their survivors may take any action permitted under the Wisconsin Business Corporation Law. A shareholder position may be comprised of three or fewer co-owners.

Wyoming: Under Wyoming law, one or more persons may act as the incorporator or incorporators of a corporation by delivering the articles of incorporation to the secretary of state for filing.

What does liability for pre-incorporation mean?

Activities by a corporation prior to filing the articles of incorporation are prohibited since they are of no force or effect. The company, or individuals on behalf of a company, may not transact business until the articles of incorporation have been filed with the secretary of state and until the organizational meeting has been conducted for the purpose of formalizing the corporate activities.

What are the filing requirements of a new corporation?

Alabama: In Alabama, the articles of incorporation must be directed to the honorable probate judge of the county in which the incorporators intend to conduct business. Pursuant to Section 10-2A-91 of the Code of Alabama as amended, the probate judge will then determine if the articles are appropriate and will see that same are filed with the secretary of state.

Alaska: In Alaska, the articles of incorporation for a new company must be directed to the Commissioner of Commerce and Economic Development of the State of Alaska. Organization for a new corporation is governed pursuant to Section 10.06.208 of the Alaska statutes, as amended.

Arizona: Articles of incorporation must be filed by both domestic and foreign corporations and the place(s) of business, and an authorized agent must be identified to the state's corporation commission. Suits may be maintained in either the county where the agent is found or where the cause of action arises.

Special laws regulate banking and insurance corporations. The shareholders or stockholders of such companies may be held individually responsible for contracts, debts, and the engagement of such corporations. Officers, directors, managers, and cashiers of corporate banking institutions may be individually responsible under certain conditions relative to insolvency or failing circumstances.

Monopolies and certain trusts are not allowed nor is any corporate activity that would, in any manner, fix prices, limit production, or regulate the transportation of a product. It is unlawful for any corporation to make contributions of money or anything of value for the purpose of influencing any election or official action. Other corporate activities are regulated under the General Corporation Law of the state of Arizona. (See Sections 10-001 through 10-1223). The corporate commission, which finds its basis under Article XV of the Arizona Constitution, has the power to supervise and investigate certain corporations and corporate activities, including any corporation whose stock is offered for sale to the public or any public service corporation.

The General Corporation Law of Arizona is divided into various articles, including Article 1—Substantive Provision; Article 2—Incorporation; Article 3—Amendments; Article 4—Merger or Consolidation; Article 5—Sale of Business; Article 6—Dissenter's Rights; Article 7—Voluntary Dissolution and Liquidation; Article 8—Involuntary Dissolution; Article 9—Foreign Corporations; Article 10—Reports and Filings; Article 11—Penalties and Liabilities; Article 12—General Provisions; Article 13—Close Corporations; Article 14—Unclaimed Shares and Dividends; Article 15—Corporation's Sale; and Article 18—Business Trusts. Information for general corporation law may be found in Sections 10-002, 10-053, 10-058, 10-071, 10-078, 10-080, 10-082, 10-094, 10-106, 10-125, 10-135, 10-137, 10-201, 10-401, 10-421, 10-451, 10-481, and 10-501. Particular nonprofit applications are found in Sections 10-701, 10-751, 10-801, and 10-821. Special provisions for professional corporations are found in Section 10-901. An additional governing regulation for business development corporations is found in Section 10-951. Special provisions that apply to nonprofit corporations may be found in Sections 10-1001, 10-1028, 10-1033, 10-1038, 10-1044, 10-1045, 10-1051, 10-1063, 10-1081, 10-1086, 10-1088, and 10-1121. Special provisions for corporate takeovers may be found in Sections 10-1201, 10-1211, and 10-1221.

Arkansas: In Arkansas, one or more persons may act as the incorporator or incorporators of a corporation by delivering articles of incorporation to the secretary of state for filing. The articles of incorporation must set forth a corporation name, the number of shares the corporation is authorized to issue, and whether or not there is a single or more than one class of stock. It should also be stated as to whether or not the shares are issued with or without par value. If the shares are divided into a number of classes, the number of shares of each class must be stated, as well as the par value of each such class or that such shares are without par value. The initial registered office and the name of the registered agent must be provided with the current street address. The name and address of each incorporator must be included in the articles of incorporation, and the primary purpose or purposes for which the corporation is organized may be stated; however, it will limit the broad purposes provided in §4-27-301 of the Arkansas Code.

California: In California, one or more natural persons, partnerships, associations, or corporations, domestic or foreign, may form a corporation under Division 1 of Title 1 of the California Corporation Code by executing and filing articles of incorporation. If initial directors are named in the articles, each director named shall sign and acknowledge the articles. If the individual directors are not named, the articles shall be signed by one or more of the incorporators. Corporate existence begins when the articles are filed with the secretary of state. The corporate existence shall be perpetual unless otherwise provided in the bylaws or so stated in the articles.

The secretary of state will not accept articles where the corporation's name is deceptive or misleading. The use of the terms "bank," "trust," "trustee," or related words are prohibited unless there has been appropriate approval by the superintendent of banks.

Colorado: In order to incorporate in Colorado, it is necessary to file certain articles of incorporation with the secretary of state. The articles of incorporation must contain a corporate name that must include the word "Corporation," "Incorporated," "Company," or "Limited," or the abbreviation "Corp.,"

"Inc.," "Co.," or "Ltd." and must be otherwise in compliance with Title 7 of the Colorado revised statutes.

Connecticut: A certificate of incorporation in Connecticut shall set forth the name of the corporation, the nature of business to be transacted, or the purpose to be promoted or carried out. It shall be sufficient to state either a loan or with other business or purpose, that the purpose of the corporation is to engage in any lawful act or activity as permitted under corporation laws, and by such statement all lawful acts and activities shall be within the purpose of the corporation. The certificate of incorporation shall also indicate the designation of each class of shares, the authorized number of shares of each class with the par value for each share, and the authorized number of shares in each class plus the terms, limitations, and relative rights regarding any preference of shares in series thereof. The minimum amount of stated capital with which the corporation shall commence business shall also be stated. The certificate of incorporation shall set forth the period, if any, for which there is a limitation on the corporation existence and shall also set forth any special provision under which the corporation is organized.

The certificate of incorporation may include any provisions not prohibited by law for the regulation and management of the affairs of the corporation for defining and regulating the powers of the corporation, its officers, directors, and shareholders or any class of shareholders. A provision may be permitted limiting the personal liability of directors to the corporation or shareholders from monetary damages for breach of duty as a director. This provision shall limit the liability to an amount that is not less than the compensation received by the director for serving the corporation during the year in which a violation or breach may have occurred. This provision would apply providing the breach did not (1) involve a knowing and comparable act in violation of the law or (2) enable the director and associate, as defined by subdivision (3) of Section 33-374d, to receive an improper personal economic gain or to show a lack of good faith and a conscious disregard for the duty of the director to the corporation under the circumstances in which the director was aware that his or her conduct or omission created an unjustifiable risk to the corporation or constituted a sustained and unexcused pattern of inattention.

Delaware: In Delaware, any person, partnership, association, or corporation without regard to residence, domicile, or state of incorporation may incorporate or establish an organization by filing a certificate of incorporation executed pursuant to Section 103 of the General Corporation Law. This certificate must be filed with the Division of Corporations in the Department of State.

Florida: All filings must be with the Department of State. The document must contain specific provisions of the Florida Business Corporation's Act, although other information may be included as well. The document must be typewritten or printed and must be in the English language. The corporate name may not be in English letters or Arabic or Roman numerals, and the certificate of status required of foreign corporations need not be in English, if accompanied by a reasonably authentic English translation. The document must be executed by the chairman or vice chairman, the board of directors, or by its president or another officer. If directors have not been selected or if a corporation has not been formed, then it must be signed by the incorporator. If the corporation is in the hands of a receiver, trustee, or other court-appointed fiduciary, it must be signed by the fiduciary. Whoever signs the document must sign it and state beneath or opposite the signature the name and capacity under which he or she signs. The document may contain a corporate seal. If there is specifically a prescribed form under Section 607.0121, the document must be in or on that prescribed form. Finally, the document must be delivered to the office of the Department of State for filing and must be accompanied by the appropriate filing fee.

Georgia: Any corporation document filed with the secretary of state must be executed by the CEO, president, or officer of the corporation unless directors have not been selected, in which case the incorporators must execute the document. If the company is in the hands of a receiver, trustee, or other court-appointed fiduciary, that fiduciary must sign. Accompanying the signature should be the identity of the person and capacity under which he or she signs. The document may contain the corporate seal, the attestation by the secretary or assistant secretary, and acknowledgment. The document filed with the secretary of state should be accompanied by one exact or conformed copy plus the correct filing fee and any specific certificate that may be required.

The secretary of state may prescribe and furnish, on request, forms for an application for a certificate of existence, a foreign corporation application for certificate of authority to transact business in Georgia, a foreign corporation's application for a certificate to withdraw, the annual registration, and other particular forms.

Hawaii: The document must first be sent to the director of the Department of Commerce and Consumer Affairs. Once the document is delivered to the director of the Department of Commerce and Consumer Affairs, the director will stamp the word "filed" and the date of the delivery on the document.

Idaho: In order to incorporate in Idaho, it is necessary to file certain articles of incorporation with the secretary of state.

Illinois: All corporate filings must be made with the secretary of state of Illinois. The secretary issues a certificate for incorporation, which is evidence of corporate existence in Illinois.

Indiana: Filing with the secretary of state in Indiana is regulated pursuant to Section 23-1-18-1. Filing must contain information required by the articles. The document must be typewritten or printed and must be in the English language. It also must be executed by the chairman of the board of directors and must be signed with the name and the capacity of the person signing. The document then must be delivered to the office of the secretary of state for filing and must be accompanied by exact or conformed copy. The correct filing fee must also be paid pursuant to Section 23-1-18-3. The fee for filing articles is $90.00.

Iowa: In order to incorporate in Iowa, it is necessary to file certain articles of incorporation with the secretary of state.

Kansas: Pursuant to Article 60, formation of a corporation may occur when any person, partnership, association, or corporation, singly or jointly with the other, forms a corporation. The corporation may be established for any lawful purpose. In this regard, see Section 17.6001.

Kentucky: All corporate documents in Kentucky must be filed with the secretary of state.

Louisiana: The articles of incorporation, or multiple originals thereof, must be filed with the secretary of state together with the actual report pursuant to R.S. 12:101. The names of the directors and addresses must appear thereon. The secretary of state then files the articles. After determining that all matters have been properly filed, the secretary of state issues a certificate of corporate existence. Then, thirty days after multiple original articles are copied and certified by the secretary of state, the articles must be filed for record in the office of the recorder of mortgages for the parish in which the registered office of the corporation is located. Under Section 26, as a "condition precedent to doing business," the corporation may not incur any debts until the amount of capital with which it will begin business has been paid in full.

Maine: The articles of incorporation must be filed with the secretary of state. The beginning of corporate existence occurs once the filed articles have been approved by the secretary of state. Once the articles have been approved by the secretary of state, an organizational meeting shall take place for the purpose of electing the board of directors and adopting bylaws.

Maryland: The Maryland General Corporation Law requires that in order for a charter document to be effective, it must be filed with the "Department." The "Department" means the State Department of Assessments and Taxations.

Massachusetts: In the commonwealth of Massachusetts, the secretary of state has the duty and obligation to examine each document submitted under the provisions of Chapter 156B for filing purposes. If the secretary of state determines that proper compliance is met, the secretary of state will keep the record of the filing and keep the documents and files in a manner convenient for public review and inspection. The secretary of state shall cause a photographic or other copy to be made of the articles of organization and amendments thereof as filed, showing his or her approval endorsed thereon and shall deliver the same to the corporation.

Michigan: In order to incorporate in Michigan, one or more persons must file articles of incorporation with the "Administrator" under Section 21.200(131). The document filed under this Michigan Business Corporation Act is effectuated by delivering the document to the administrator, together with the fees and accompanying documents required by law. The administrator then marks the document "filed," signs with his or her title, and provides the date received and filed. The documents must be filed in the English language.

Minnesota: Documents filed with the secretary of state in the state of Minnesota require that the documents be in the English language. The corporate name must be made up of letters and characters of the English language as well. The documents should be executed by the incorporators and verified. An indication of the person's title should also appear, and if mandatory forms are required, the mandatory forms should be filed as well.

Mississippi: Documents for incorporation in the state of Mississippi must be filed with the secretary of state. Documents filed with the secretary of state must be typewritten or printed in black ink and must be in the English language. The capacity in which a person signs must be identified. The document must be delivered to the secretary of state accompanied with one exact or conformed copy, along with the appropriate fees and taxes. A document accepted for filing is effective at the time of filing on the date it is filed, as evidenced by the secretary's endorsement on the original document, or at the time specified in the document. A delayed effective time and date may be specified. The secretary of state, upon filing, stamps the word "filed" together with his or her name and official title and the date and time of receipt upon the document. The secretary of state then, upon request, furnishes a certificate of existence for a domestic corporation or a certificate of authority for a foreign corporation.

Missouri: The filing requirements are that the document be typewritten or printed in the English language and executed by the chairman of the board or the president or another officer. A capacity under which a person signs must be stated beneath the signature. Corporate existence would begin at the time of filing on the date filed as evidenced by the secretary of state's date and time endorsement, or the document may specify a later date for its commencement of activities.

Montana: The filing requirements in the state of Montana require compliance with Chapter 1 of Title 35, which is known as the Montana Business Corporation Act. The articles must be typewritten or printed and must be in the English language.

Nebraska: The incorporators, on behalf of the corporation, shall conduct the preliminary meeting and shall function as the board of directors until the first meeting, at which time the various officers and board of directors may be selected. The incorporators must call the first meeting for organizational purposes. An original and a duplicate copy of the articles must be filed with the secretary of state. The name of the corporation must be in the English language, and the articles must be typewritten or printed. After filing with the secretary of state, the duplicate copy shall be recorded in the office of the county clerk in the county where the registered office of the corporation is located in Nebraska.

Nevada: In order to incorporate in the state of Nevada, it is necessary to file articles of incorporation with the secretary of state. One or more natural persons may associate with each other to form a corporation for the transaction of any lawful business or to promote or conduct any legitimate object or purpose, pursuant to and subject to Chapter 78. The articles must conform with Section 78.035 and must be filed with the secretary of state.

New Hampshire: The articles of incorporation must be filed with the secretary of state by sending duplicate originals of the articles to the secretary. Upon the delivery and the tender of the required filing fee, the secretary of state will endorse each of the duplicate originals with the word "filed" and the month, day, and year of the filing. Such an endorsement is known as the "filing date" of the articles of incorporation and is conclusive proof of the date and time of filing. The secretary of state will record one of the duplicate originals in the secretary's office and issue a certificate from the corporation to which the secretary will affix the duplicate original. The certificate of incorporation together with the duplicate original of the articles of incorporation attached to the certificate by the secretary shall be returned to the incorporators or their representative.

New Jersey: Documents relating to corporations in the state of New Jersey must be filed with the secretary of state. The documents must be in the English language in English letters or Arabic or Roman numerals. The documents that are to be filed are to be delivered to the secretary of state with the proper fees and any required accompanying documents. The secretary of state will endorse the document with the word "filed" along with the secretary's official title and the date of filing with the secretary's office. The effective date is the time of filing, unless a later date is specified, so long as that date is within thirty days after the date of filing. The document shall be signed by the chairman of the board, or the president, or a vice president. The name of the person and the capacity under which he or she signs must also be specified.

New Mexico: In New Mexico, there exists the State Corporation Commission, which is operated by a chief clerk. Each corporation (if not exempted) must file in the office of the State Corporation Commission within thirty days after the date on which its certificate of incorporation or its authority is issued by the commission. Biannually thereafter, on or before the fifteenth day of the third month following the end of the corporation's taxable year, it must file a corporate report in the form prescribed and furnished to the corporation. Such report must show (1) current status of the corporation, (2) mailing address and street address of its registered office in New Mexico and the name of the agent, (3) names and addresses of all the directors and officers of the corporation and when the term of office of each expires, (4) the character of the corporate business and principal place of business (address of registered office in the state or country under the laws of which it was incorporated and the principal office), and (5) the date of the next annual meeting. The report must also disclose the status as of the last day of the taxable year, the amounts of the authorized shares, the value and location of the property, the gross receipts derived from business and property in the state, the balance sheet of the corporation's financial condition, as well as the corporation taxpayer identification numbers.

New York: Every certificate of incorporation that is delivered to the Department of State of the state of New York for filing must be in the English language. The corporate name may be in another language if written, however, in the English language or characters. Original documents must be filed and signed and delivered to the Department of State.

North Carolina: Documents relating to corporations in North Carolina must be filed with the secretary of state. They must be typewritten or printed and must be in the English language. The corporate name need not be in English if written in English letters or Arabic or Roman numerals. The effective date of any document is the date the document is filed, as evidenced by the secretary of state's date and time endorsement on the original document.

North Dakota: Unless a later date is specified for the corporate existence of a corporation in North Dakota, its existence begins when the articles of incorporation are filed with the secretary of state.

Ohio: In Ohio, a corporation must be filed with the secretary of state, and compliance must be met with Section 1701 et. seq. The information must be typewritten or printed and must be in the English language. The documents, such as articles of incorporation, must be signed by the incorporators prior to filing with the secretary of state.

Oklahoma: In Oklahoma, the certificate of incorporation must be filed with the secretary of state. The certificate must be in compliance with the Business Corporation Act of Oklahoma. It must be executed, acknowledged, and filed with a duplicate copy delivered to the office of the secretary of state, along with the appropriate filing fee. Any corporate franchise tax as authorized by law to be collected by the Oklahoma Tax Commission shall be tender to the Oklahoma Tax Commission.

Oregon: Corporate documents in the state of Oregon must be filed with the secretary of state. The document must be in the English language. The document must be executed by either the chairman of the board of directors, its president, or another of its officers. If the directors have not yet been selected, it should be executed by an incorporator. If the corporation is in the hands of a trustee, receiver, or other court appointed fiduciary, that fiduciary should execute the document filed with the secretary of state. The person who signs the documents to be filed with the secretary of state must state the capacity under which he or she signs.

Pennsylvania: Filing requirements of the commonwealth of Pennsylvania request that the documents such as the articles of incorporation be submitted in triplicate. The name of the corporation shall be set forth, along with a post office address. The act of assembly or authority by which the company was organized or incorporated should also be noted. A statement regarding the nature of the business should be set forth. The name and residence of the company treasurer must be stated. Also, the Department of State shall note the fact and date of the issuance of the certificate of incorporation.

Rhode Island: The filing of articles of incorporation must be done according to Section 7-1.1-49 by filing duplicate originals. The duplicate originals should be delivered to the secretary of state. If everything is in order, the secretary of state will endorse each duplicate original with the word "filed." A copy of one of the original duplicates is kept at the office of the secretary of state while the other original duplicate is returned to the individual incorporators with the issued certificate of incorporation. After the issuance of the certificate of incorporation, the majority of the directors may call an organizational meeting for the purpose of conducting business and outlining the business procedures of the corporation.

South Carolina: The filing of corporate documents is done through the office of the secretary of state in South Carolina. The filing must comply with the information required by Chapters 1 through 20 of Title 22 of the South Carolina statutes. The articles for incorporation must be typewritten or printed and must be in the English language. The name of the corporation must be in English letters or Arabic or Roman numerals. The document must be executed by the chairman of the board or the president of the new company. If there are no directors, then the articles of incorporation must be signed by the incorporators or by a fiduciary if the corporation is in the hands of a receiver, a trustee, or some other fiduciary. The articles of incorporation must be signed by the incorporators and the individuals signing them must state the title under which each individual signs the articles. If a mandatory form is required under the laws of South Carolina, the mandatory form must be used. The document then must be delivered to the secretary of state and accompanied by one exact or conformed copy. Of course, the correct filing fees must be provided at the time of filing with the secretary of state.

South Dakota: Filings must be accomplished with the secretary of state with the original plus an exact or conforming copy of the articles of incorporation. All appropriate filing fees that need to be paid should also accompany the original and exact copy of the articles filed with the secretary of state. The secretary of state shall then endorse the word "filed" on the original or the exact copy with the month, day, and year of filing. The secretary of state will file the original in his or her office and issue a certificate of incorporation.

Tennessee: A corporation in the state of Tennessee may be established by a document that is typewritten in the English language. The corporation name must be written in English letters or Arabic or Roman numerals. The document must be executed by the president or other authorized officers.

Texas: In Texas, a corporation must be filed with the secretary of state and compliance must be met with the Texas Business Corporation Act. The filing of the articles is through the secretary of state, who endorses the word "filed" on the original. Although the original document remains in the office of the secretary of state, a certificate of incorporation will be issued.

Utah: An original and one copy of the articles of incorporation shall be delivered to the Division of Corporations and Commercial Code. If that division finds that the articles of incorporation conform to law, it will then, when fees have been paid as prescribed in Title 16, endorse on the original and one copy the word "filed" and the month, day, and year of the filing. The original shall be filed in the office of Division of Corporations and Commercial Code, and the certificate of incorporation shall be issued.

Vermont: The filing requirements for a new corporation in Vermont are covered under Section 1.20. Specific forms may be prescribed by the secretary of state, pursuant to Section 1.21. The filing fees are set forth in Section 1.22.

Virginia: The filing requirements in the commonwealth of Virginia for the articles of incorporation are found in Section 13.1-604. A document must be provided satisfying the requirements of the section and any other section that adds to or varies from the requirements that must be filed with the commission. The document shall be one that the chapter requires or permits to be filed with the commission, and the document shall contain the information required by the chapter. It may contain additional information as noted, particularly in Section 13.1-619. The document shall be typewritten or printed. The typewritten or printed portion shall be in black, and manually assigned photocopies or other reproduced copies of typewritten or printed documents may be filed. The document shall be in the English language; however, the corporate name need not be in English, if written in English letters or Arabic or Roman numerals. The articles of a foreign corporation need not be in English if accompanied by a reasonably authenticated English translation. The document shall be executed in the name of the corporation. The individual executing the document shall sign it and state beneath or opposite his or her signature the name and capacity under which each signs. If the commission has prescribed a mandatory form to be used, then such form must be used as requested by the commission.

Washington: Certificate of existence or authorization is one that is issued by the secretary of state upon the proper filing of the articles of incorporation.

West Virginia: The secretary of state of West Virginia is constituted as the attorney-in-fact for, and on behalf of, every corporation created by virtue of the laws of West Virginia. Articles of incorporation must be filed with the secretary of state, who will certify the filing. Each set of articles of incorporation must be filed as duplicate originals. (Both copies must be executed in the original form.) The articles must be delivered to the secretary of state for filing. The secretary will endorse upon each duplicate original the word "filed," along with the month, day, and year of the filing. One original shall be kept in the secretary's office. The secretary will issue a certificate of incorporation to which the other original will be affixed. If the corporation is a domestic corporation, it shall cause its certificate or certified copy of the certificate to be recorded in the clerk of the county commissioner of the county in which the corporation's principal office is located. (See Section 31-1-28.)

Wisconsin: Filing in Wisconsin must be accomplished through the secretary of state's office. The document must be delivered to the secretary of state's office for filing, along with the appropriate filing fee. Documents filed with the secretary of state shall be executed by an officer of the corporation. However, if a board of directors has not been selected, an incorporator must sign. If the corporation is in the hands of a receiver, trustee, or court-appointed fiduciary, the fiduciary must sign. The capacity in which a person signs must also be stated. A document filed by the secretary of state under Wisconsin Business Corporation Law is effective on the date that it is received by the office of the secretary of state for filing at (1) the time of day specified in the document or (2), if no time is specified, at the close of business.

Wyoming: All documents relating to corporations in Wyoming must be filed with the secretary of state. The document must be typewritten or printed. It shall be in the English language. However, the corporate name may be in another language so long as it is written in English letters or Arabic or Roman numerals. The document must be executed by the chairman of the board of directors or by its president or by another officer. However, if a president or officers have not been elected or selected, the document must be executed by an incorporator. If the corporation is in the hands of a receiver, trustee, or a fiduciary appointed by the court, it must be exercised by that fiduciary.

Certain specific forms may be required by the secretary of state. Examples of such forms include the application for a certificate of existence and a foreign corporation's application for a certificate of authority to transact business in Wyoming. A foreign corporation is any corporation that has not been incorporated in Wyoming.

What are the guidelines for determining the corporate name?

Alabama: In Alabama, the corporate name shall include the word "Corporation" or "Incorporated," or shall contain an abbreviation of such words. Banking corporations shall use the words "bank," "banking," or "bankers." The name cannot be deceptively similar to that of another company. Some exceptions with particular written consent might apply.

Alaska: The corporate name of a company in Alaska must contain within the name the word "Corporation," "Incorporated," "Company," or "Limited," or the abbreviation of any of those four words. Language must not be used in the corporate name that would indicate an identity that is deceptively similar to the name of another corporation.

Arizona: The corporate name of each corporation organized under the laws of Arizona must contain one of the following words: "Association," "Bank," "Corporation," "Company," "Incorporated," or "Limited." The corporate name, in lieu of the foregoing words, may have an abbreviation of any of those words. The corporation's name must not be deceptive in any respect such that the corporation would include the name "Bank" and not be organized for banking purposes. In other words, if a corporation uses the word "Bank," it must be in the banking business and must comply with the other laws that apply to banking in Arizona.

Arkansas: In Arkansas, the corporate name must contain the word "Corporation," "Incorporated," "Company," or "Limited," or the abbreviation "Corp.," "Inc.," "Co.," or "Ltd.," or words or abbreviations of like import in another language. The corporation may not contain language stating or implying that the corporation is organized for a purpose other than those contained in §4-27-301 and its articles of incorporation. A corporation name must be distinguishable from other corporate names authorized to do business and transact business in the state of Arkansas or other corporate names registered under §4-27-402 or §4-27-403. It is possible to register the name of the foreign corporation. It is also possible to have the use of fictitious names (§4-27-404), in addition to the corporation name in Arkansas. The change of registered office or registered agent must be done in compliance with §4-27-503.

California: The secretary of state will not accept articles where the corporation name is deceptively similar or misleading in reference to an already existing name or name of another entity. The use of the terms "Bank," "Trust," "Trustee," or related words are prohibited unless there has been an appropriate approval by the superintendent of banks.

Colorado: The articles of incorporation must contain a corporate name that includes the word "Corporation," "Incorporated," "Company," or "Limited," or an abbreviation of one of those words, and must be otherwise in compliance with Title 7 of the Colorado revised statutes.

Connecticut: Section 33-286 deals with the restrictions or purposes and powers of the corporation and should be reviewed to determine the full extent of corporate use of the state of Connecticut. Section 33-287 provides that the corporate name must include the word "Corporation," "Company," "Incorporated," "Limited," or "Societa de zoning Azinoi," "or the abbreviation "Corp.," "Co.," "Inc.," "Ltd.," or "SpA."

Delaware: The certificate of incorporation must contain one of the following words: "Association," "Company," "Corporation," "Club," "Foundation," "Fund," "Incorporated," "Institute," "Society," "Union," "Syndicate," or "Limited," or it must contain one of the following abbreviations: "Co.," "Corp.," "Inc.," "Ltd.," or words or abbreviations of like import in other languages so long as they are written in Roman character or letters.

Florida: The corporate name must contain the word "Corporation," "Company," or "Incorporated," or the abbreviation of one of those words or abbreviations of like import of another language that will clearly indicate that it is a corporation instead of a natural person or partnership. The articles may not contain language sustaining or implying that the corporation is organized for a purpose other than that permitted by the Florida law or by its own articles of incorporation. The corporate name may not contain language stating or implying that the corporation is connected with a state or federal government agency or chartered under the laws of the United States. The corporate name must be distinguishable from the names of all other entities or companies organized, registered, or reserved under the state of Florida and on file with the Division of Corporations.

Georgia: The name of the corporation in Georgia must contain the word "Corporation," "Incorporated," "Company," or "Limited," or the abbreviation "Corp.," "Inc.," "Co.," or "Ltd." It may not contain anything obscene nor be more than eighty characters including space and punctuation.

Hawaii: In conjunction with Section 415-58, the corporate name must include the word "Corporation," "Incorporated," or "Limited," or the abbreviations "Corp.," "Inc.," or "Ltd." The corporation name may not be deceptively similar to any other name already existing.

Idaho: The corporate name must contain the word "Corporation," "Company," "Incorporated," or "Limited," or the abbreviation "Corp.," "Co.," "Inc.," or "Ltd." In the event the word "Company" or its abbreviation is used, it shall *not* be immediately preceded by the word "and" or an abbreviation or symbol for the word "and." There may not be any names used that are the same or deceptively similar to names of already existing corporations.

Illinois: The name of each company must contain the word "Corporation," "Company," "Incorporated," or "Limited," or abbreviations of any of the foregoing. Once corporate existence has commenced, the board of directors shall have an initial organizational meeting at which time the appropriate bylaws regarding the regulation of the company may be approved. The bylaws may contain provisions regarding the regulation and management of the affairs of the corporation not inconsistent with law or the articles of incorporation. A company in Illinois may be organized for any lawful purpose. The articles of incorporation may limit the actual purpose of the corporation so desired.

Indiana: The corporation name must contain the word "Corporation," "Incorporated," "Company," or "Limited," or the abbreviation "Corp.," "Inc.," "Co.," or "Ltd."

Each corporation in the state of Indiana must continuously maintain a registered office and a registered agent who must be an individual residing in Indiana or a domestic corporation whose business is identical with the registered office or a foreign corporation whose business office is identical with the registered office.

Iowa: In order to incorporate in Iowa, it is necessary to file with the secretary of state certain articles of incorporation. The articles of incorporation must contain a corporate name that must include the word "Corporation," "Incorporated," "Company," or "Limited," or the abbreviation "Corp.," "Inc.," "Co.," or "Ltd." and must be otherwise in compliance with Section 490.401 of the Code of Iowa. A corporate name may not be deceptively similar to an entity already in existence and operating in the state of Iowa.

Kansas: Contained within the articles of incorporation and as provided in Section 17.6002, the name (except for banks) should include the word "Association," "Church," "College," "Company," "Corporation," "Club," "Foundation," "Fund," "Incorporated," "Institute," "Society," "Union," "Syndicate," or "Limited," or the abbreviation "Co.," "Corp.," "Inc.," or "Ltd."

Kentucky: A corporate name in Kentucky must contain the word "Corporation," "Incorporated," "Company," or "Limited," or the abbreviation "Corp.," "Inc.," "Co.," or "Ltd." The name may not imply activity other than Section 271B.3-010 or other than permitted under the articles of incorporation. The corporate name must be distinguishable from other names recorded by the secretary of state.

Louisiana: A corporation in the state of Louisiana, except in the cases of railroad, telegraph, and telephone corporations, shall contain the word "Corporation," "Incorporated," or "Limited, or the abbreviation "Corp.," "Inc.," or "Ltd." The new corporation may contain the word "Company" and its abbreviation "Co." if it is not immediately preceded by the word "and" or the symbol "&." The articles must be in English language, signed by each incorporator or his or her agent, and acknowledged by the one who signed.

Maine: Under the Maine Business Corporation Act, the corporate name must not contain any word or phrase that indicates that the corporate purpose is different that the purposes allowed under the act. The name may not be deceptively similar to any already existing domestic or foreign corporation, reserved name, trademark, or other registered mark unless authorized. The corporate name must also be different from any domestic or foreign limited partnership.

Maryland: The corporate name should include either one of the following or an abbreviation of the following: "Company," if not preceded by the word "and" or a symbol "&"; "Corporation"; "Incorporated"; or "Limited."

Massachusetts: The corporate name must contain the word "Corporation," "Company," "Incorporated," or "Limited," or the abbreviation "Corp.," "Co.," "Inc.," or "Ltd." In the event the word "Company" or its abbreviation is used, it shall *not* be immediately preceded by the word "and" and/or an abbreviation or symbol for the word "and." There may not be any names used that are the same or deceptively similar to those of corporations already existing.

Michigan: In order to incorporate in Michigan, it is necessary to file the articles with the administrator, along with the corporate name, which must include the word "Corporation," "Incorporated," "Company," or "Limited," or the abbreviation "Corp.," "Inc.," "Co.," or "Ltd." and must be otherwise in compliance with Section 21.200(211) of the Michigan Business Corporation Act.

Minnesota: Contained within the corporate name must be language, letters, or characters in the English language. Also, the corporate name must contain the word "Corporation," "Incorporated," "Limited," or "Company," or the abbreviations "Corp.," "Inc.," or "Ltd." If "Co." is used, it may not be preceded by the word "and" or the symbol "&." A corporation may not imply a purpose different than that for which it is incorporated, and it may not use a name that is deceptively similar to a name that is already in existence.

Mississippi: In Mississippi, the corporate name must contain the word "Corporation," the abbreviation "Corp.," the word "Incorporated," the abbreviation "Inc.," the word "Company," the abbreviation "Co.," the word "Limited," or the abbreviation "Ltd."

Missouri: The name of a company in Missouri must include the word "Corporation," "Company," "Incorporated," "Limited," or an abbreviation of those identifying words. No word implying that the company is a government agency shall be permitted, and no word or name that is deceptively similar to another company or entity existing in the state of Missouri may be used.

Montana: The articles of incorporation must contain a corporate name that must include the word "Corporation," "Incorporated," "Company," or "Limited," or the abbreviation "Corp.," "Inc.," "Co.," or "Ltd." and must be otherwise in compliance with Section 35-1-301 of the Code of Montana. The corporate name may not have any word or phrase that implies any purpose other than the one for which the company is organized. The corporate name may not be deceptively similar to another name already in existence.

Nebraska: The corporate name for a company in Nebraska shall contain the word "Corporation," "Company," "Incorporated," or "Limited," or an abbreviation of one of those four words. The corporation, under Section 21-2007, may not imply a different purpose than that for which it is incorporated, and the name may not be deceptively similar to another corporation already in existence in the state.

Nevada: The company name may not appear to be that of a natural person or a continuing given name or initials except, however, the additional word or words including "Incorporated," "Limited," "Company," or "Corporation." The abbreviations "Inc.," "Ltd.," "Co.," or "Corp." may be used, or other words that identify the company as not being a natural person.

New Hampshire: The corporate name in New Hampshire shall include the word "Corporation," "Incorporated," or "Limited," or shall contain an abbreviation of one of these words. The corporate name shall not contain any word or phrase that indicates or implies that it is organized for any purpose other than the one stated in the articles of incorporation. In addition, it shall not be the same or deceptively similar to any name of a domestic corporation existing under the laws of the state of New Hampshire or any foreign corporation authorized to transact business in New Hampshire.

New Jersey: A corporation may be organized in New Jersey for any lawful purpose except any business that is otherwise regulated by another statute of the state, unless such statute permits organization under Title 14A. The corporate name shall not contain any word or phrases or abbreviations that indicate or imply that the corporation is organized for any purpose other than one that is permitted by its certificate of incorporation. The name may not be confusingly similar to another corporate name, and it may not contain a word or phrase or abbreviation that is prohibited or restricted by law unless in compliance with such restrictions.

New Mexico: The name of a corporation in New Mexico must include one of the followding words: "Corporation," "Incorporated," "Company," "Association," "Club," "Society," "Union," "Syndicate," or the abbreviation "Co.," or "Inc." The corporate existence shall begin after the filing date with the Corporate Commission.

New York: In New York, a corporation name must include: "Corporation," "Incorporated," or "Limited," or an abbreviation of one of those three words.

The corporation shall not contain any of the following phrases or abbreviations of the following phrases:

board of trade	state police
chamber of commerce	state trooper
community renewal	tenant relocation
urban relocation	urban development

Additionally, the corporation name must not contain any of the following words or abbreviations or derivations thereof:

acceptance	indemnity
annuity	insurance
assurance	investment
bank	lawyer
benefit	loan
bond	mortgage
casualty	savings
doctor	surety
endowment	title
fidelity	trust
finance	underwriter

North Carolina: A corporate name in North Carolina must contain the word "Corporation," "Incorporated," "Company," or "Limited," or the abbreviations "Corp.," "Inc.," "Co.," or "Ltd." The corporate name may not imply any purpose other than that for which the corporation is organized, and the name must be distinguishable from any other corporations pursuant to Section 55-4-01 of the North Carolina Business Corporation Act.

North Dakota: The corporate name must be in the English language and must contain the word "Corporation," "Incorporated," or "Limited," or the abbreviation "Corp.," "Inc.," or "Ltd." Or, the name may contain the word "Company" or abbreviation "Co.," so long as "Company" or "Co." is not preceded by the word "and" or the symbol "&." The corporate name may not be deceptively similar to another name that is used for another corporation as registered under the laws of the state of North Dakota.

Ohio: The name of the corporation must include the word "Company," "Corporation," or "Incorporated" or the abbreviation "Co.," "Corp.," or "Inc." The company name may not imply that a government agency is involved, and it must not be indistinguishably similar in name to a company that is already in existence.

Oklahoma: A corporation name in the certificate of incorporation shall contain one or more of the following words: Association, Company, Corporation, Club, Foundation, Fund, Incorporated, Institute, Society, Union, Syndicate, or Limited. The company may include the following abbreviations: Co., Corp., Inc., or Ltd.

The name of the corporation may also contain words of like import. A corporation in Oklahoma must be distinguishable from names of other corporations, foreign corporations, names of partnerships, of limited partnerships, of trade names, fictitious names filed with the secretary of state, and any corporate or limited partnership names reserved with the secretary of state.

Oregon: Section 60.094 regulates the type of name that may be used for corporations in the state of Oregon. A corporate name must include one of the following: "Corporation," "Incorporated," "Company," or "Limited," or an abbreviation of any of the foregoing. A corporate name shall not contain the word "Cooperative." The corporation name must also be written in the alphabet used to write the English language. It must not be deceptively similar to another corporate name, reserve name, business name, trust name, partnership name, etc.

Pennsylvania: A proper corporate name for a business corporation in the state of Pennsylvania shall include one of the following corporate designators: "Corporation" or "Corp.," "Company" or "Co.," "Incorporated" or "Inc.," "Limited" or "Ltd.," "Association," "Fund," or "Syndicate," and words or abbreviations of like import in languages other than English. The word "Company" or "Co." may be immediately preceded by "and" or "&," whether or not they are immediately followed by one of the words "Incorporated," "Inc.," "Limited" or "Ltd." For example, John Doe & Co. The corporate name shall also comply with the applicable requirements of Chapter 17 (relating to names).

Rhode Island: A corporate name in Rhode Island must include the word "Corporation," "Company," "Incorporated," or "Limited." The abbreviations "Corp.," "Co.," "Inc.," or "Ltd." may also be used.

South Carolina: The corporate name of a company in South Carolina must contain within the corporate name the words "Corporation," "Incorporated," "Company," or "Limited," or the abbreviation "Corp.," "Inc.," "Co.," or "Ltd." A name of a company may not contain language stating or implying that the corporation is organized for a purpose other than that permitted by Section 33-3-101. A company name may not be deceptively similar to the name of a corporation already doing business in the state. Also, the name may not be similar to a corporate name which is reserved for the name of a foreign corporation or the name of a not-for-profit corporation.

South Dakota: A corporate name under the state of South Dakota is governed by Section 47-2-36. Any corporate name, except a nonprofit corporation, must include the word "Corporation," "Incorporated," "Company," or "Limited," or an abbreviation of any of those four words. A company name may not be deceptively similar to another name already in use by a domestic corporation, a corporation that has registered a name, or by a foreign corporation. The corporate name must be translated into English or must be in English.

Tennessee: A corporate name must include the word "Corporation," "Incorporated," "Company," or "Limited," or the abbreviations "Corp.," "Inc.," "Co.," or "Ltd." Certain language may not be contained in the corporate name. (See particularly Section 48-14-101.)

Texas: The corporation name must include the word "Corporation," "Company," or "Incorporated," or one of the following abbreviations: "Corp.," "Co.," or "Inc."

Utah: In Utah, a corporation's name must include the word "Corporation," "Company," or "Incorporated," or the abbreviation "Corp.," "Co.," or "Inc.," or words or abbreviations of like import in another language. Only the names of corporations may contain the word "Corporation" or "Incorporated" or the abbreviation "Corp." or "Inc." A corporate name may not contain any language stating or implying that the corporation is organized for a purpose other than that permitted by Subsection (4) and by its articles of incorporation. The corporation name must be distinguishable from other corporations or other corporate names reserved, including fictitious names adopted by foreign corporations or any corporations not for profit.

Vermont: A corporation in the state of Vermont must contain one of the following words: "Corporation," "Incorporated," "Company," or "Limited." If the name of the corporation does not include one of the foregoing words, it may include one of the following abbreviations: "Corp.," "Inc.," "Co.," or "Ltd." A corporation's name may not contain language stating or implying that the corporation is organized for a purpose other than that permitted by Section 301 of Title 11A and the articles of incorporation. The corporation may not have a similar name or a name that is deceptively similar to or confused with or mistaken for the name of companies or reserved names or fictitious names or nonprofit names or the names of foreign corporations that have registered in the state of Vermont. It is possible to reserve a name for a corporation under Section 4.02 in the state. It is recommended that a foreign corporation doing business in the state of Vermont register as such. A registered name for a foreign corporation is covered by Section 4.03.

Virginia: A corporation may not have a name that is deceptively similar to a name of another company, and it must be otherwise in compliance with the laws of the commonwealth of Virginia, particularly Chapter 9 of Title 13.

Washington: A corporate name in the state of Washington must include one of the following words: "Corporation," "Incorporated," "Company," or "Limited." In lieu of any of the foregoing names, the following abbreviations may be used: "Corp.," "Inc.," "Co.," or "Ltd." The name of a company may not be deceptively similar to another corporation already organized under the laws of the state of Washington. It is possible to register a name, in the state of Washington, under Section 23B.04.030 or to reserve a name under Section 23B.04.020.

West Virginia: The name of a corporation in West Virginia shall contain the word "Corporation," "Company," "Incorporated," or "Limited," or an abbreviation of such words. The name of the corporation shall not contain any word or phrase that indicates or implies that it is organized for any purpose other than one or more of the purposes contained in its articles of incorporation. The name may not be the same or deceptively similar to the name of any other corporation and shall be translated into letters of the English alphabet, if not in the English language.

Wisconsin: The corporate name for a company in Wisconsin must include the word "Corporation," "Incorporated," "Company," or "Limited." The corporate name, as an alternative, may include the abbreviation "Corp.," "Inc.," "Co.," or "Ltd." The corporate name must not include language that indicates it is organized for any purpose other than that stated in its bylaws and articles and as permitted by law. The name may not be deceptively similar to another name being used by another corporation, partnership, or other entity in Wisconsin. (See Section 180.0401.)

Wyoming: In Wyoming, a corporate name is intended to include any name so long as it does not imply a purpose other than that permitted by W.S. 17-16-301. The name may not be deceptively similar to that of any other corporation, trade name, trademark, partnership, limited partnership, etc.

What is the purpose of a corporation?

A company may be incorporated for any purpose in most states so long as the purpose is lawful. The articles of incorporation may limit the actual purpose of the corporation, if so desired.

What are the articles of incorporation?

Articles of incorporation or a certificate of incorporation represents the official document of organization for a new company. The articles of incorporation must be executed and filed in duplicate and signed by the incorporators. The articles must set forth the corporation name; the purpose for which the corporation is organized (this may be a statement that the corporation is organized for any or all lawful businesses); the address of the initial registered officer; the name of the initial registered agent; the name and address of each incorporator; the number of shares of each class of stock; the number and class of shares that the corporation proposes to issue without further report to the secretary of state (in some cases the document will need to be filed with a commissioner of economic development, local probate judge, or other government officials); the designation of each class of stock and a statement of the designation, preferences, qualification, limitations, restrictions, and special or relative rights; and if the corporation may issue the shares of any preferred or special class in series. The articles may also set forth the names and addresses of the initial board of directors; provisions regarding the management of the business and the regulation of the affairs of the corporation; limitations on the rights, powers, and duties of the corporation, its officers, directors, and shareholders; the limitation of preemptive rights; an estimate of the value of property held by the corporation; and special voting provisions. The corporate articles may also place limitation on the personal liability of the directors or shareholders.

The corporate existence begins when a certificate of incorporation is issued by the secretary of state. The certificate of existence will be issued by the secretary of state upon complete compliance with the relevant statute and the filing of the appropriate and approved articles of incorporation.

What are the bylaws of a corporation?

The bylaws of a corporation are the rules and regulations of the corporation. A set of bylaws should be in place in order for each of the shareholders to understand their rights as well as the rights of the various board members and officers. It is recommended that the bylaws be active at the time of the organizational meeting.

What is meant by "corporate records"?

Corporate records should be maintained by each new corporation. The officers of the corporation should maintain the control and updates of the record of minutes, the articles, the bylaws, and other official documents of the corporation that have been filed with the secretary of state that authorize the company to do business. Generally, the secretary of the corporation maintains these records and would make them available to all shareholders at times of reasonable request.

What is a corporate book?

Generally, when a corporation is organized, a corporate book or corporate file box is prepared by the attorney. The book or corporate box is usually divided into various sections, including a section for official documents, which might contain the certificate of incorporation, the articles of incorporation, any Election of Assumed Name, any filings with other states, secretary of state filings, and trade names, as well as any other official document. The second section generally contains the minutes of the proceedings of the meetings of the corporation. Included within the minutes are the general organizational meeting minutes, the minutes for the board of directors' meetings, and the minutes for the shareholders' meetings, which generally occur at least once annually. The third section involves the corporate treasury and often contains a general ledger, shareholders' ledger, a record of the names of the shareholders, the payments made by them to the corporation for the stock received, the number of shares held, and the stock certificate number. The reports of the treasurer of the corporation will also appear in this section. A contract section is also generally included and reflects the various contracts into which the corporation has entered for one purpose or another. Finally, there is usually a correspondence section, which reflects the correspondence of the officers of the corporation and the administration of corporate business.

What does "capitalization" mean?

Every corporation organized for operation in the state of Illinois should be adequately capitalized. Capitalization will assure corporate operations and permit the corporation to function as a viable entity. Scrutiny may be given to the adequacy of capitalization by various taxing authorities or individuals or entities who, for some reason or another, may wish to pierce the corporate veil in the event there is a belief that the corporation was established as a sham and without proper or adequate capitalization. The articles of incorporation must describe the various classes of shares and the number of shares of each class that the corporation is authorized to issue.

What are the rights of a corporation in real estate transactions?

A corporation generally has the same rights to engage in the purchase and sale of real estate. However, certain requirements are relative to real estate transactions, which must be met. An attorney should be consulted relative to any conveyances.

What is the purpose of the organizational meeting?

An organizational meeting must be conducted subsequent to the receipt of the articles of incorporation from the secretary of state or other appropriate government official. The purpose of the organizational meeting is to commence the operations of the company. Such commencement of operations includes the formulation of bylaws, the election of a board of directors, and the election of officers.

Is a stock certificate necessary?

Certain restrictions may be applied to the transfer of stock, and in many cases those restrictions must be placed upon the certificate itself. Various forms of certificates are acceptable; however, it should be stated upon the certificate that the stock was issued pursuant to a particular state and under the laws of that state.

The corporation may issue shares of stock with or without certificates, and in such cases the corporations must send the shareholders a written statement of the information required on the certificates. At minimum, each share certificate should contain on its face the name of the issuing corporation and the laws under which it is organized, the name of the person to whom the share is issued, the number and class of shares issued, and the designation of the series, if any, that the certificate represents. If different classes of shares or different series within a class are permitted, then the designation's relative rights, preferences, and limitations applicable to each class plus the variations and rights, preferences, and limitations determined for each series, and the authority of the board of directors to determine such variations for future series must be summarized on the front or back of each certificate. In the alternative, the certificates may state conspicuously that the corporation will furnish the shareholder such information in writing and without charge. Also, each share certificate must be signed either manually or in facsimile by two officers designated in the bylaws or by the board of directors, and the certificates may bear the corporate seal or a facsimile of the seal of the corporation.

When must I file corporate documents?

In order for a document such as the articles of incorporation to be acceptable to the secretary of state or other appropriate officer, the document must be accepted for filing at the time filing is made with the secretary or officer. Once the secretary or officer accepts and files the document, the secretary or officer will affix the word "filed," along with his or her name and title.

Samples

Although samples of various forms are provided in the following text for your review, it is important to be mindful that these samples are examples that may or may not be applicable or satisfactory for your individual needs. Therefore, it is important to keep in mind that the "samples" provided should be reviewed with an attorney in order to ascertain their complete and proper usage.

Many of the duties, rights, and obligations of individuals becoming shareholders of the corporation involve complex legal issues and involve various laws that have evolved over a substantial period of time during which many changes have been made. Accordingly, it is very important that an individual who seeks to incorporate properly and wishes to have his or her rights properly protected consult an attorney. The attorney should be an individual who is experienced in the dealings of corporate law and who is familiar with not only the incorporation process for the particular state in question but is also familiar with various tax consequences. In this regard, the attorney consulted should be in a position to advise the incorporating parties and/or prospective shareholders on the consequences of closely held corporations, "C" and "S" corporations, the requirements for Subchapter S filing status, and other federal tax information, including the federal tax identification number application.

CHAPTER • 4

Sample Forms

The sample forms in this chapter are completed with fictitious information in order to illustrate how the forms should be completed. Opposite each page of the sample form are end notes, which correspond to the filled-in information in the completed sample form. This chapter illustrates how to use the blank forms in Chapter 5. The chapters may be used together by matching the sample form (in Chapter 4) to the corresponding blank form in Chapter 5.

Sample Form
ARTICLES[1] OF INCORPORATION
OF EXETOR COMPANY[2]

TO THE SECRETARY OF STATE[3] OF THE STATE OF ILLINOIS[4]:

The undersigned persons, acting as incorporators of a corporation organized pursuant to the Illinois Business Corporation Act of 1963, Chapter 805[5], as amended, hereby adopt the following Articles of Incorporation.

ARTICLE I

NAME: The name of the corporation under Chapter 805[6] shall be known as: EXETOR COMPANY[7].

ARTICLE II

PERIOD OF DURATION: The period of duration of Exetor Company[8] shall be perpetual unless dissolved under the laws of the State of Illinois[9] or changed in accordance with these Articles and the corporation Bylaws.

ARTICLE III

PURPOSE: This corporation is organized for the purpose of conducting proper aspects of business in a manner in which the corporation was organized for operation under Chapter 805[10] of the Illinois Business Corporation Act of 1963[11] as amended, with the principal purpose of engaging in real estate acquisitions with the principal interest on nursing homes and care facilities[12].

ARTICLE IV

AGGREGATE SHARES: The aggregate number of shares which the corporation is authorized to issue is 1,000,000[13], consisting of one class with no[14] par value. The voting rights will be exercised in direct relation to the number of shares held by the single class established.

ARTICLE V

REGISTERED OFFICE/AGENT: The address of the initial office of the corporation shall be 123 Main Street, Chicago, Illinois[15]. The name of its initial registered agent at said address is Elmer Dolby[16] pursuant to Section 5/5.05[17].

The form opposite is an example of how a typical form for the Articles of Incorporation may be completed. A blank version of this form (for your use) appears on pages 105–107.

1. The Articles of Incorporation as used, must be filed with the appropriate governing agency, such as the state of Illinois. In some states, such as New Jersey, this document is called the Certificate of Incorporation; therefore, an attorney should be consulted as to the proper usage or terminology.

2. This should be the company name. Be sure to check with the appropriate authority, such as the Secretary of State, to determine whether or not the name chosen for the company is not already in use by some other entity and be certain that the name is not restricted by banking laws or insurance laws.

3. The appropriate government official in the case of Illinois is the secretary of state. However, in some states, such as Alaska, it may be the Commissioner of Economic Development, or it may be the local probate judge, such as in the state of Alabama.

4. The state where the articles are to be filed.

5. The name of the state corporation act or other particular statute, the appropriate year in which the particular state statute was enacted and the particular chapter or section under which a corporation is organized in a given state shall be provided in this space.

6. The particular chapter under which a corporate name may be authorized in a state.

7. The name of the company.

8. The name of the company.

9. The state.

10. The appropriate chapter or section of the business corporation law of that particular state.

11. The state and the legislative enactment.

12. The purpose for the corporation. In this case nursing homes is used only as an example.

13. Number of shares to be issued by the corporation. The use of 1,000,000 is arbitrary.

14. The amount of par value per share. In the example above, no par is shown; however, the par value per stock may be any agreed amount.

15. Address of the corporation's registered office, along with the city and state.

16. The name of the registered agent at the registered office.

17. The section of the state code that governs the registered office and registered agent.

Sample Form: Articles of Incorporation of Exetor Company *(continued)*

ARTICLE VI

BOARD OF DIRECTORS: The number of directors constituting the initial Board of Directors will be <u>three</u>[18] and each shall serve as director until his successor is elected and qualifies under the Bylaws of the corporation. After the initial Board of Directors, the Board shall consist of such number of directors as shall be fixed and/or determined by the shareholders from time to time at each annual meeting thereof, at which time the directors are to be elected. The initial directors of the new corporation shall be the undersigned incorporators.

ARTICLE VII

BYLAWS: The Bylaws of <u>Exetor Company</u>[19] may contain any restrictions on the transfer of the shares of stock of the corporation as well as the issuance of any bonds or notes.

ARTICLE VIII

CORPORATE EXISTENCE: The corporation's existence shall begin on the day these <u>Articles</u>[20] are filed with the <u>Secretary of State</u>[21] and recorded at the office of the <u>Cook</u>[22] County Recorder.

ARTICLE IX

INCORPORATORS: The names and addresses of the incorporators are:

<u>Elmer Dolby</u>[23]   /s/_____ [23]
<u>123 Main Street</u>
<u>Chicago, Illinois</u>

<u>Richard Snull</u>[24]   /s/_____ [24]
<u>333 High Cliff Drive</u>
<u>Chicago, Illinois</u>

<u>David Hokey</u>[25]   /s/_____ [25]
<u>987 Swimmer Lane</u>
<u>Chicago, Illinois</u>

The form opposite is an example of how a typical form for the Articles of Incorporation may be completed.

18. The arbitrary number of three (3) was chosen in this case for the number of people to serve on the Board of Directors; however, generally any number may be used. The reader is reminded that a controllable number of directors is recommended.

19. Name of the company.

20. Articles, Certificates, or other nomenclature, whichever is suggested by a particular state to identify this document.

21. Secretary of State or some such other office as designated by state statute, such as Commissioner of Economic Development as in Alaska or to the probate judge of the local county in the case of Alabama.

22. Not always does a state require that the document be filed with the county recorder's office; however, in this case we have chosen to do so.

23. Name and address of incorporator along with his or her signature opposite his or her name as shown.

24. Name and address of incorporator along with his or her signature opposite his or her name as shown.

25. Name and address of incorporator along with his or her signature opposite his or her name as shown.

Sample Form: Articles of Incorporation of Exetor Company *(continued)*

STATE OF ILLINOIS[26]   )

)ss

COUNTY OF COOK[27]   )

On this 5th[28] day of April[28], 1996[28], before me, the undersigned Notary Public, personally appeared Elmer Dolby[29], Richard Snull[29] and David Hokey[29] to me known to be the persons named in and who executed the foregoing Articles of Incorporation and they acknowledged that they executed the same as their voluntary act and deed.

                            _____

                            NOTARY PUBLIC[30]

The form opposite is an example of how a typical form for the Articles of Incorporation may be completed.

26. The state of Illinois has been chosen in this case; however, in appropriate verification, the necessary state must be included as well as the county where the document was signed.

27. County in which the document is signed.

28. An arbitrary date has been selected in the above example; however, the date the document is signed by the incorporators before the notary needs to be included.

29. Names of the individual incorporators need to be indicated as they appear before the notary.

30. Signature of the Notary Public.

Sample Form
BYLAWS (4 OFFICERS)
OF <u>EXETOR COMPANY</u>[1]

ARTICLE I. PRINCIPAL OFFICE

The principal office of the corporation in the State of <u>Illinois</u>[2] shall be located in the City of <u>Chicago</u>[3], County of <u>Cook</u>[4]. The corporation may have such other offices, either within or without the State of <u>Illinois</u>[5], as the Board of Directors may designate or as the business of the corporation may require from time to time (<u>pursuant to Section 5/5.05</u>[6]).

ARTICLE II. SHAREHOLDERS

SECTION 1. <u>ANNUAL MEETING.</u> The annual meeting of the shareholders shall be held in the last week of <u>April</u>[7] of each year, beginning in <u>1996</u>[8] for the purpose of electing Directors and for the transaction of such other business as may come before the meeting. If the day fixed for the annual meeting shall be a legal holiday in the State of <u>Illinois</u>[9], such meeting shall be held on the next succeeding business day. If the election of Directors shall not be held on the day designated herein for any annual meeting of the shareholders, or any adjournment thereof, the Board of Directors shall cause the election to be held at a special meeting of the shareholders as soon thereafter as conveniently possible (<u>pursuant to Section 5/7.05</u>[10]).

SECTION 2. <u>SPECIAL MEETINGS.</u> Special meetings of the shareholders, for any purpose or purposes, unless otherwise prescribed by statute, may be called by the President or by the Board of Directors, and shall be called by the President at the request of two shareholders (<u>pursuant to Section 5/705</u>[11]).

SECTION 3. <u>PLACE OF MEETING.</u> The Board of Directors may designate any place, either within or without the State of <u>Illinois</u>[12], as the place of meeting for any annual meeting or for any special meeting called by the Board of Directors. A waiver of notice signed by all shareholders entitled to vote at a meeting may designate any place, either within or without the State of <u>Illinois</u>[13], unless otherwise prescribed by statute, as the place for the holding of such meeting. If no designation is made, or if a special meeting is otherwise called, the place of meeting shall be the principal office of the corporation in the State of <u>Illinois</u>[14].

SECTION 4. <u>NOTICE OF MEETING.</u> Written notice stating the place, day and hour of the meeting and, in case of special meeting, the purpose or purposes for which the meeting is called, unless otherwise prescribed by statute, shall be delivered not less than <u>10</u>[15] nor more than <u>60</u>[16] days before the date of the meeting, either personally or by mail, by or at the direction of the <u>President</u>[17], or the <u>Secretary</u>[18], or the persons calling the meeting, to each shareholder of record entitled to vote at such meeting. If mailed, such notice shall

The form opposite is an example of how a typical form for the Bylaws may be completed. A blank version of this form (for your use) appears on pages 109–114.

1. The name of the company. The sample name used in the previous examples is also used here to show consistency.

2. The State of Illinois is provided to show consistency and to make the Bylaws applicable to Illinois.

3. The city.

4. The county.

5. The state.

6. The appropriate code section in Illinois is shown; however, the code sections of other states can be completed by your attorney should he or she wish to include those sections. Otherwise, the section may be deleted altogether.

7. The month of April was chosen arbitrarily as the month for the annual meeting.

8. The 1996 date was chosen since that was the date of this publication.

9. The state.

10. The reference to a code section is optional. You may or may not wish to include it.

11. The reference to a code section is optional. You may or may not wish to include it.

12. The State of Illinois was used as an example pursuant to the preceding samples prepared for your reference.

13. The State of Illinois was used as an example pursuant to the preceding samples prepared for your reference.

14. The State of Illinois was used as an example pursuant to the preceding samples prepared for your reference.

15. The number 10 was used as an arbitrary period of time; however, often state statutes require a minimum period of time for notice.

16. As to 60 days, that was also arbitrarily selected; however, often states will require a different time.

17. The President was selected as the typical officer to be identified regarding notice; however, another officer may be designated under the Bylaws.

18. The Secretary was selected as the typical officer to be identified regarding notice; however, another officer may be designated under the Bylaws.

Sample Form: Bylaws (4 Officers) of Exetor Company *(continued)*

be deemed to be delivered when deposited in the United States mail, addressed to the shareholder at his address as it appears on the stock transfer books of the corporation, with postage thereon prepaid (pursuant to Section 5/7.15 and Section 5/7.20[19]).

SECTION 5. QUORUM. A majority of the outstanding shares of the corporation entitled to vote, represented in person or by proxy, shall constitute a quorum at a meeting of shareholders. If less than the outstanding shares are represented at a meeting, a majority of the shares so represented may adjourn the meeting from time to time without further notice. At such adjourned meeting at which a quorum shall be present or represented, any business may be transacted which might have been transacted at the meeting as originally noticed. The shareholders present at a duly organized meeting may continue to transact business until adjournment, notwithstanding the withdrawal of enough shareholders to leave less than a quorum (pursuant to Section 5/7.60[20]).

SECTION 6. PROXIES. At all meetings of shareholders, a shareholder may vote in person or by proxy executed in writing by the shareholder or by his duly authorized attorney in fact. Such proxy shall be filed with the Secretary[21] of the corporation before or at the time of the meeting. No proxy shall be valid after four weeks from the date of its execution, unless otherwise provided in the proxy (pursuant to Section 5/7.50 and 5/7.55[22]).

SECTION 7. VOTING OF SHARES. Subject to the provisions of any language to the contrary of this Article II, each outstanding share entitled to vote shall be entitled to one vote upon each matter submitted to a vote at the meeting of the shareholders (pursuant to Section 5/5.30, 5/7.65 and 5/7.70[23]).

SECTION 8. CUMULATIVE VOTING. Unless otherwise provided by law, at each election for Directors, every shareholder entitled to vote at such election shall have the right to vote, in person or by proxy, the number of shares owned by him for as many persons as there are Directors to be elected and for whose election he has a right to vote, or to cumulate his votes by giving one candidate as many votes as the number of such Directors multiplied by the number of his shares equal, or by distributing such votes on the same principle among any number of candidates (pursuant to Section 5/5.30, 5/7.65 and 5/7.70[24]).

ARTICLE III. BOARD OF DIRECTORS

SECTION 1. GENERAL POWERS. The business and affairs of the corporation shall be managed by its Board of Directors (pursuant to Section 5/8.05[25]).

SECTION 2. NUMBER, TENURE AND QUALIFICATIONS. The number of Directors of the corporation shall be four[26]. Each Director shall hold office until the next annual meeting of shareholders and until his successor shall have been elected and qualified (pursuant to Section 5/8.10[27]).

The form opposite is an example of how a typical form for the Bylaws may be completed.

19. The reference to a code section is optional.

20. The reference to a code section is optional.

21. The office of Secretary was chosen for this form; however, another officer could be designated.

22. The reference to a particular code section is optional based upon the discretion of the attorney and/or client.

23. The reference to a particular code section is optional based upon the discretion of the attorney and/or client.

24. The reference to a particular code section is optional based upon the discretion of the attorney and/or client.

25. The reference to a particular code section is optional based upon the discretion of the attorney and/or client.

26. The number four (4) is an arbitrary number, and in the particular sample shown, four (4) directors were chosen. It is possible for the shareholders to decide that a reasonable number of directors may be voted into office for the purpose of making up the board of directors.

27. The reference to a particular code section is optional based upon the discretion of the attorney and/or client.

Sample Form: Bylaws (4 Officers) of Exetor Company *(continued)*

SECTION 3. <u>REGULAR MEETING.</u> A regular meeting of the Board of Directors shall be held without other notice than this Bylaw immediately after, and at the same place as, the annual meeting of shareholders. The Board of Directors may provide, by resolution, the time and place for the holding of additional regular meetings without other notice than such resolution (<u>pursuant to Section 5/8.20</u>[28]).

SECTION 4. <u>SPECIAL MEETING.</u> Special meetings of the Board of Directors may be called by or at the request of the President or any two directors. The person or persons authorized to call special meetings of the Board of Directors may fix the place for the holding of any special meeting of the Board of Directors called by them (<u>pursuant to Section 5/8.20</u>[29]).

SECTION 5. <u>NOTICE.</u> Notice of any special meeting shall be given at least three days previously thereto by written notice delivered personally or <u>mailed to each director at his business address, or by telegram</u>[30].

SECTION 6. <u>QUORUM.</u> A majority of the number of directors is two and shall constitute a quorum for the transaction of business at any meeting of the Board of Directors (<u>pursuant to Section 5/8.15</u>[31]).

SECTION 7. <u>MANNER OF ACTING.</u> The act of the majority of the directors present at a meeting at which a quorum is present shall be the act of the Board of Directors.

SECTION 8. <u>ACTION WITHOUT A MEETING.</u> Any action that may be taken by the Board of Directors at a meeting may be taken without a meeting if a consent in writing, setting forth the action so to be taken, shall be signed before such action by all of the directors(<u>pursuant to Section 5/8.45</u>[32]).

SECTION 9. <u>VACANCIES.</u> Any vacancy occurring on the Board of Directors may be filled by the affirmative vote of a majority of the remaining directors, though less than a quorum of the Board of Directors, unless otherwise provided by law. A director elected to fill a vacancy shall be elected for the unexpired term of his predecessor in office. Any directorship to be filled by reason of an increase in the number of directors may be filled by election by the Board of Directors for a term of office continuing only until the next election of Directors by the shareholders (<u>pursuant to Section 8.30</u>[33]).

ARTICLE IV. OFFICERS

SECTION 1. <u>NUMBER.</u> The officers of the corporation shall be <u>four</u>[34]. A <u>President, Vice President, Secretary and Treasurer</u>[35], each of whom shall be elected by the Board of Directors. Such other officers and assistant officers as may be deemed necessary may be elected or appointed by the Board of Directors from time to time (<u>pursuant to Section 5/8.50</u>[36]).

The form opposite is an example of how a typical form for the Bylaws may be completed.

28. The reference to a particular code section is optional based upon the discretion of the attorney and/or client.

29. The reference to a particular code section is optional based upon the discretion of the attorney and/or client.

30. The method of service was chosen particularly for this notice; however, different states may require different forms of notice and/or the incorporators and shareholders may require a different form of notice. The form of notice should be set forth pursuant to the laws of the particular state in which you incorporate and the desire of the shareholders.

31. The reference to a particular code section is optional based upon the discretion of the attorney and/or client.

32. The reference to a particular code section is optional based upon the discretion of the attorney and/or client.

33. The reference to a particular code section is optional based upon the discretion of the attorney and/or client.

34. The number of officers shall be stated.

35. Other officers may be included such as the First Vice President of Finance, the First Vice President of Marketing, the First Vice President of Sales, etc. However, in this model and the above example, four (4) officers are being shown.

36. The reference to a particular code section is optional based upon the discretion of the attorney and/or client.

Sample Form: Bylaws (4 Officers) of Exetor Company *(continued)*

SECTION 2. <u>ELECTION AND TERM OF OFFICE.</u> The officers of the corporation shall be elected annually by the Board of Directors and such election shall be held after each annual meeting of the shareholders. If the election of officers shall not be held at the meetings of the Board of Directors annually, such election shall be held as soon thereafter as conveniently possible. Each officer shall hold office until his successor shall have been duly elected and shall have qualified, or until his death or until he shall resign or shall have been removed in the manner hereinafter provided (<u>pursuant to Section 5/8.50</u>[37]).

SECTION 3. <u>REMOVAL.</u> Any officer or agent may be removed by the Board of Directors whenever, in its judgment, the best interests of the corporation will be served thereby, but such removal shall be without prejudice to the contract rights, if any, of the person so removed. Election or appointment of an officer or agent shall not of itself create contract rights(<u>pursuant to Section 5/8.55</u>[38]).

SECTION 4. <u>VACANCIES.</u> A vacancy in any office because of death, resignation, removal, disqualification or otherwise, may be filled by the Board of Directors for the unexpired portion of the term (<u>pursuant to Section 5/8.30</u>[39]).

SECTION 5. <u>PRESIDENT</u>[40]. The President shall be the principal executive officer of the corporation and, subject to the control of the Board of Directors, shall supervise and control all of the business and affairs of the corporation. He shall, when present, preside at all meetings of the shareholders and of the Board of Directors. He may sign, with the Secretary or any other proper officer of the corporation thereunto authorized by the Board of Directors, certificates for shares of the corporation, any deeds, mortgages, bonds, contracts or other instruments which the Board of Directors has authorized to be executed. He may not sign in cases where the signing and execution thereof shall be expressly delegated by the Board of Directors or by these Bylaws to some other officer or agent of the corporation, or shall be required by law to be otherwise signed or executed; and, in general, the President shall perform all duties incident to the office of President and such of the duties as may be prescribed by the Board of Directors from time to time.

SECTION 6. <u>VICE PRESIDENT</u>[41]. In the absence of the President or in event of his death, inability or refusal to act, the Vice President shall perform the duties of the President and, when so acting, shall have all the powers of and be subject to all the restrictions upon the President. The Vice President shall perform such other duties as from time to time may be assigned to him by the President or by the Board of Directors.

SECTION 7. <u>SECRETARY</u>[42]. The Secretary shall: (a) keep the minutes of the proceedings of the shareholders and of the Board of Directors in one or more books provided for that purpose; (b) see that all notices are duly given in accordance with the provisions of these Bylaws or as required by law; (c) be custodian of the corporate records of the corporation;

The form opposite is an example of how a typical form for the Bylaws may be completed.

37. The reference to a particular code section is optional based upon the discretion of the attorney and/or client.

38. The reference to a particular code section is optional based upon the discretion of the attorney and/or client.

39. The reference to a particular code section is optional based upon the discretion of the attorney and/or client.

40. Other duties and functions may be delineated as to a President; however, the ones included are standard.

41. Other duties and functions may be delineated as to a Vice President; however, the ones included are standard.

42. Other duties and functions may be delineated as to a Secretary; however, the ones included are standard.

Sample Form: Bylaws (4 Officers) of Exetor Company *(continued)*

(d) keep a register of the post office address of each shareholder which shall be furnished to the Secretary by such shareholder; (e) sign with the President, certificates for shares of the corporation, the issuance of which shall have been authorized by resolution of the Board of Directors; (f) have general charge of the stock transfer books of the corporation; (g) in general, perform all duties incident to the officer of Secretary and such other duties as from time to time may be assigned to him by the President or by the Board of Directors.

SECTION 8. <u>TREASURER</u>[43]. The Treasurer shall (a) have charge and custody of, and be responsible for, all funds and securities of the corporation; (b) receive and give receipts for monies due and payable to the corporation from any source whatsoever, and deposit all such monies in the name of the corporation in such banks, trust companies or other depositories as shall be selected; and (c) in general, perform all of the duties incident to the officer of Treasurer and such other duties as from time to time may be assigned to him by the President or by the Board of Directors.

SECTION 9. <u>SALARIES</u>[44]. The salaries of the officers shall be fixed from time to time by the Board of Directors and no officer shall be prevented from receiving such salary by reason of the fact that he is also a director of the corporation.

ARTICLE V. CONTRACTS, LOANS, CHECKS AND DEPOSITS

SECTION 1. <u>CONTRACTS</u>[45]. The Board of Directors may authorize any officer or officers, agent or agents, to enter into any contract or execute and deliver any instrument in the name of and on behalf of the corporation, and such authority may be general or confined to specific instances.

SECTION 2. <u>LOANS</u>[46]. No loans shall be contracted on behalf of the corporation and no evidence of indebtedness shall be issued in its name unless authorized by a resolution of the Board of Directors. Such authority may be general or confined to specific instances.

SECTION 3. <u>CHECKS, DRAFTS, ETC.</u>[47] All checks, drafts or other orders for the payment of money, notes or other evidences of indebtedness issued in the name of the corporation, shall be signed by such officer or officers, agent or agents of the corporation and in such manner as shall from time to time be determined by resolution of the Board of Directors.

SECTION 4. <u>DEPOSITS</u>[48]. All funds of the corporation not otherwise employed shall be deposited from time to time to the credit of the corporation in such banks, trust companies or other depositories as the Board of Directors may select.

ARTICLE VI. CERTIFICATES FOR SHARES AND THEIR TRANSFER

SECTION 1. <u>CERTIFICATES FOR SHARES</u>[49]. Certificates representing shares of the corporation shall be in such form as shall be determined by the Board of Directors.

The form opposite is an example of how a typical form for the Bylaws may be completed.

43. Other duties and functions may be delineated as to a Treasurer; however, the ones included are standard.

44. Various amounts of salaries may be set or formulas may be used to set forth salaries; however, the typical language for Bylaws has been included.

45. The matter of contracts may be more specific; however, fundamentally, at least the language used should be provided.

46. The matter of contracts may be more specific; however, fundamentally, at least the language used should be provided.

47. As to checks, drafts, etc., arbitrarily we have selected that this language be used to allow a resolution to be passed by the Board of Directors which would indicate who would sign the checks. Oftentimes, the Bylaws may require that two (2) officers sign the checks if the amount is over a specific sum.

48. Generally, any officers or shareholders are permitted to make deposits.

49. Each state has different laws that regulate the issuance of stock certificates. Generally, the certificates are signed by the President and Secretary; however, that does not have to be the case. Other officers may be designated to be the individuals signing the certificates, and often the case is for the Treasurer to sign the certificates. The language contained in this sample is generic; therefore, for specific language relating to a given state, an attorney should be consulted.

Sample Form: Bylaws (4 Officers) of Exetor Company *(continued)*

Such certificates shall be signed by the President and by the Secretary. All certificates for shares shall be consecutively numbered or otherwise identified. The name and address of the person to whom the shares represented thereby are issued, with the number of shares and date of issue, shall be entered in the stock transfer books of the corporation. All certificates surrendered to the corporation for transfer shall be canceled and no new certificate shall be issued until the former certificate for a like number of shares shall have been surrendered and canceled. In case of a lost, destroyed or mutilated certificate, a new one may be issued upon such terms and indemnity to the corporation as the Board of Directors may prescribe (pursuant to Section 5/6.05, 5/6.10, 5/6.15, 5/6.25 and 5/6.30[50]).

SECTION 2. TRANSFER OF SHARES. Transfer of shares of the corporation shall be made only on the stock transfer books of the corporation by the holder of record thereof or by his legal representative, who shall furnish proper evidence of authority to transfer, or by his attorney thereunto authorized by Power of Attorney duly executed and filed with the Secretary of the corporation, and on surrender for cancellation of the certificate for such shares. The person in whose name the shares stand on the books of the corporation shall be deemed by the corporation to be the owner thereof for all purposes. Any such transfers may be governed by specific restriction on the face of the certificate[51].

ARTICLE VII. AMENDMENTS

These Bylaws may be altered, amended or repealed, and new Bylaws may be adopted by the Board of Directors at any regular or special meeting of the Board of Directors.

ARTICLE VIII. RATIFICATION OF ACTS[52]

The directors and officers of this corporation shall not be personally liable to the corporation or its stockholders for monetary damages for breach of fiduciary duty as a director, except for liability to the extent provided by applicable law (i) for any breach of the director's duty of loyalty to the corporation or its stockholders, (ii) for acts or omissions not in good faith or which involve intentional misconduct or knowing violation of the law, (iii) for any transaction from which the director derived an improper personal benefit, or (iv) under state law. No amendment to or repeal of this Article shall apply to or have any effect on the liability or alleged liability of any director of the corporation for or with respect to any acts or omissions of such director occurring prior to such amendment or repeal. The directors of this corporation have agreed to serve as directors in reliance upon the provisions of this Article.

The form opposite is an example of how a typical form for the Bylaws may be completed.

50. An appropriate code section may or may not be included.

51. The transfers relative to stock, in this particular case, have a restriction that must appear on the face of the certificate if restriction is mandated or required by either the shareholder or the Board of Directors. Many times the company may wish to have a specific restriction on the transfer of stock, especially if the corporation is a Subchapter S or a closely held corporation. In such cases, it is recommended that specific language relative to the restriction of the transfer of stock be placed not only in the Bylaws, but also in a stock retirement or cross purchase agreement. A sample agreement to Restrict Transfer of Stock is contained within this booklet as a sample form.

52. Often corporations will want to assure the officers and directors of the corporation that they do not incur personal liability as a result of their acting on behalf of the corporation so long as their actions are within the realm of the Bylaws and other authority which are conveyed to them by virtue of their office with the company. Many times the part of the Articles of Incorporation will contain similar language to the language contained in the sample Bylaws. On the other hand, many times a provision relative to Ratification of Acts is not included. It is both a matter of choice by the shareholders and a matter of state laws.

Sample Form
<u>EXETOR COMPANY</u>[1] CHECKLIST
<u>FEDERAL ID #421116987</u>[2]
(Date Notation of Various Filing)

	1996	1997	1998
Federal Income Tax Return	<u>April 14</u>[3]		
Secretary of State	<u>March 1</u>[4]		
Annual Report	<u>March 15</u>[5]		
State Income Tax Return	<u>March 30</u>[6]		
Annual Meeting	<u>February 20</u>[7]		
Dividend	<u>February 20</u>[8]		

The form opposite is an example of how a typical form for the Checklist may be completed. A blank version of this form (for your use) appears on page 115.

1. The name of the company.

2. An application for a federal identification number must be submitted. A copy of a sample application is enclosed in these forms. The form must be completed for the federal taxing authorities and should be filed immediately after the appropriate government agency, such as the Secretary of State or other designated public official, receives the Articles of Incorporation or Certificate of Incorporation and files same. The Internal Revenue Service will then, in turn, provide a specific federal identification number to the corporation which will be used by the company (generally through its accountant) for the filing of tax reports each year.

3. This checklist provides a place for the date the Federal Income Tax Return is filed under each column for the years given. This allows anyone reviewing the records to be sure that the federal income taxes were filed and indicates the date when the filing occurred.

4. If a report to the Secretary of State is required, in addition to an Annual Report, this allows for the company secretary or treasurer to make a notation as to when that report was filed.

5. Most generally each state requires an Annual Report to be filed by each company. This checklist allows for a space for that notation and enables anyone reviewing the records to be certain that an Annual Report was filed by the company. An Annual Report must be filed by a company in order for the company to maintain current status in the state in which the company has been incorporated or permitted to operate.

6. Income tax for various states is generally required for corporations, and this checklist allows for a space for the state income tax return to be noted so that any of the shareholders or taxing authorities, etc. may examine the company records to determine that the state income taxes have been filed.

7. It is required in virtually every state that an Annual Meeting of the corporation occur. This checklist allows for the notation to be made as to when the Annual Meeting did occur and enables any shareholder, upon review of the records, to know when the Annual Meeting was held. As indicated elsewhere, in particular under the Bylaws, Annual Meetings require notice to the shareholders. For a suggested copy of the Notice to the shareholders, see the Form-Official Notice Annual Stockholders' Meeting in the following materials.

8. If a company declares a dividend or return on the investment of the shareholders, the dividend usually is discussed at the annual meeting of the shareholders and would no doubt have been the result of discussions of the board meeting preceding the Annual Meeting of the shareholders. This enables each of the shareholders at the Annual Meeting to understand what is paid as dividend to each shareholder during the ending fiscal year.

Sample Form:
APPLICATION FOR EMPLOYER
IDENTIFICATION NUMBER

To be filed with Internal Revenue Service

1. Name (true name as distinguished from trade name)

   EXETOR COMPANY[1]

2. Trade Name, if any (Name under which business is operated, if different from item 1)

   N/A[2]

3. Social Security Number, if sole proprietor

   N/A[3]

4. Address of principal place of business (Number and Street)

   123 Main Street[4]

   City and State   Zip

   Chicago, Illinois[4]   38167[4]

5. Ending month of accounting year

   December 31[5]

6. County of Business Location

   Cook County[6]

7. Type of organization[7]   __ Individual   __ Trust   __ Partnership

   __ Other   __ Governmental   __ Nonprofit   X_ Corporation

8. Date you acquired or started this business (Mo., day, year)

   April 1, 1996[8]

9. Reason for applying[9]

   X_ Started New Business   __ Purchased Going Business   __ Other

10. First date you paid or will pay wages for this business (Mo., day, year)

   May 1, 1996[10]

The form opposite is an example of how a typical form for the Application for Employer Identification Number may be completed. A blank version of this form (for your use) appears on pages 117–118.

1. The name of the company should be included in this blank.

2. Oftentimes companies use trade names, and although the application has a place for the trade name, appropriate protection of a trade name should be sought through legal counsel. Protection is generally accorded by an appropriate filing with the Secretary of State or some other public official.

3. This is applicable if the application applies to an individual.

4. This is self-explanatory and should include an address where mail may be received. It is not recommended to be a post office box.

5. The reason the month is important is due to the fact that many times corporations are on a fiscal rather than a calendar year. Therefore, the date of ending the fiscal year is necessary in blank 5.

6. This is self-explanatory but is necessary for the federal application.

7. This is self-explanatory but is necessary for the federal application.

8. This is self-explanatory but is necessary for the federal application.

9. This is self-explanatory but is necessary for the federal application.

10. This is self-explanatory but is necessary for the federal application.

Sample Form: Application for Employer Identification Number *(continued)*

11. Nature of business[11]

Engaging in real estate acquisitions with the principal interest on nursing homes and care facilities.

12. Do you operate more than one place of business[12]?

X Yes   __ No

13. Peak number of employees expected in next 12 months (If none, enter "0")[13]

1 Nonagricultural   0 Agricultural   1 Household

14. If nature of business is manufacturing, state principal product and raw material used.[14]

N/A

15. To whom do you sell most of your products or services[15]?

____ Business establishments   X General Public   ____ Other

16. Have you ever applied for an identification number for this or any other business[16]?

____ Yes   X No

If yes, enter name and trade name. Also enter approx. date, city, state where you applied and previous number if known.

Date[17]   Signature and Title[17]   Telephone[17]

_____   _____   _____

The form opposite is an example of how a typical form for the Application for Employer Identification Number may be completed.

11. It is not necessary to have a detailed explanation of the nature of the business; however, the basic nature of the business should be described for the federal authorities due to taxing purposes.

12. This is self-explanatory but is necessary for the federal application.

13. Three options are provided which are self-explanatory. Each has a blank for the indicated type of employee.

14. This is self-explanatory but is necessary for the federal application.

15. This is self-explanatory but is necessary for the federal application.

16. This is self-explanatory but is necessary for the federal application.

17. Be certain that the form is signed and appropriately dated and submitted to the IRS.

Sample Form
PRELIMINARY MEETING
OF <u>EXETOR COMPANY</u>[1]

On the <u>2nd</u>[2] day of <u>January</u>[2], <u>1996</u>[2], a Preliminary Meeting of the Incorporators of a new <u>Illinois</u>[3] Corporation to be known as the <u>Exetor</u>[4] Corporation was held at <u>123 Main Street</u>[5] in <u>Chicago</u>[6], Illinois. <u>Diane J. Alexander</u>[7], (legal counsel), was present. <u>Elmer Dolby</u>[8], <u>Richard Snull</u>[8] and <u>David Hokey</u>[8] were present and will serve as incorporators and as members of the original Board of Directors, along with <u>Janet Olson</u>[9] and <u>Dorothy Bennet</u>[9], who were not present.

PURPOSE: At the outset of the meeting, the general discussion related to the purpose of the new corporation which involved the full range of corporate business as with particular emphasis on <u>engaging in real estate acquisitions with the principal interest on nursing homes and care facilities</u>[10], which will be located at <u>123 Main Street, Chicago</u>[11], Illinois. The corporate existence begins subsequent to the filing of Articles of Incorporation with the <u>Secretary of State</u>[12].

REGISTERED OFFICE-AGENT-DIRECTORS: It was determined <u>Elmer Dolby</u>[13] will serve as the Registered Agent for the corporation and would use his business address at <u>123 Main Street, Chicago</u>[14], Illinois as the registered office of the corporation. In regard to the foregoing, the following resolution passed unanimously:

RESOLVED: That the new Corporation will be known as the <u>Exetor Company</u>[15] and <u>Elmer Dolby</u>[16] will serve as the Registered Agent for the corporation; the Registered Office for the corporation will be at <u>123 Main Street, Chicago</u>[17], Illinois; the original incorporators will serve as the Board of Directors; and an appropriate set of Bylaws will govern the activities of the corporation. The registered office and registered agent are represented to the Secretary of State in conjunction with <u>Illinois Code</u>[18].

BOARD MEMBERS: After the foregoing resolution passed, there was a general discussion relative to the service of Board Members and the individuals incorporating the new business. It was decided that from time to time the members of the Board of Directors would function as officials acting on behalf of the corporation and, in such capacity, the actions of the board should be the sanctioned actions of the company.

RESOLVED: All acts undertaken on behalf of the corporation by the Board of Directors shall be and are hereby ratified to be the official acts of the company in order to expedite the organization process.

The form opposite is an example of how a typical form for the Preliminary Meeting may be completed. A blank version of this form (for your use) appears on pages 119–120.

A preliminary meeting of the corporation is not a recognized act of the corporation. It should be particularly noted that until a corporation receives official status through the appropriate filing with the proper government entity (such as Secretary of State), any acts generally undertaken on behalf of the corporation may result in individual liability to the incorporators. In other words, a corporation may not act as a corporation until it has been appropriately and properly filed with the governing authority (example given, Secretary of State in the state of Illinois). Therefore, the purpose of the preliminary meeting is simply to focus the parties on the various acts that they need to complete in order for the corporation to become an official and organized entity.

1. Name of the company.

2. This should be the date on which the meeting was held for the purpose of discussing all matters as disclosed through the preliminary meeting minutes.

3. The name of the state in which filing a new corporation.

4. Name of the company.

5. An arbitrary address has been used on these forms.

6. An arbitrary state has been used on these forms.

7. Generally, it is advisable to have legal counsel present; therefore, a space has been provided for the name of legal counsel.

8. Individuals listed are the incorporators or the people who met for the purpose of incorporating.

9. The individuals who also had planned to be a part of the corporation but who are unavailable for the meeting are listed at this juncture.

10. An arbitrary statement of the purpose of this particular corporation has been stated. At this juncture, the parties will need to state the principal purpose of their new company.

11. An arbitrary location has been used on this form.

12. Since Illinois was selected as the state for this sample form, the Secretary of State is the governing authority to which the Articles of Incorporation are to be directed upon completion of same.

13. Each corporation must have a Registered Agent for the purpose of service and, otherwise, for being identified by government entities, etc. In this sample form, the name of Elmer Dolby was arbitrarily selected as the Registered Agent.

14. An arbitrary location has been used on this form.

15. Name of corporation.

16. An individual should be selected as the Registered Agent of the corporation. This individual will receive any service of process or any official notification by the Secretary of State or any government entity.

17. The location provided should be the location where all corporate matters can be retrieved and the location where all corporate matters should be sent.

18. The Registered Office and Registered Agent should be indicated to be in compliance with the appropriate state code. Here the state of Illinois was chosen.

Sample Form: Preliminary Meeting of Exetor Company *(continued)*

CAPITALIZATION: The foregoing resolution passed unanimously whereupon the total stock issue and the need for capitalization was reviewed. It was determined that approximately <u>Twenty Thousand Dollars</u>[19] <u>($20,000)</u> will be needed to start the project.

NO PAR: It was suggested that the total number of shares to be issued by the corporation be at least <u>1,000,000</u>[20] shares. Some discussion related to the value of the stock and its likelihood to appreciate or depreciate over the years. Therefore, it was suggested that the stock be issued at "<u>no par.</u>"[21] In this regard the following resolution was proposed.

RESOLVED: That the corporation be authorized to issue an aggregate of <u>1,000,000</u>[22] shares at "<u>no par.</u>"[23]

The foregoing resolution passed unanimously whereupon the next order of business was a discussion regarding the interest of various individuals in acquiring stock in the corporation. In this regard <u>Elmer Dolby</u>[24] would likely invest Dollar Amount of <u>Ten Thousand</u>[25] <u>($10,000)</u>[26] each in property interest now held. <u>Richard Snull</u>[27] discussed the likelihood of investing <u>Five Thousand</u>[28] <u>($5,000)</u>[29]. It was anticipated that each of the individuals would share in the investment made. <u>David Hokey</u>[30] indicated an interest in investing <u>Five Thousand</u>[31] <u>($5,000)</u>[32]. At an appropriate time during the next organizational meeting and/or the First Meeting of Directors a resolution would be passed for the issuance of stock in the corporation.

SMALL BUSINESS CORPORATION: It was determined that the corporation would function as a small business corporation with no more than <u>35</u>[33] shareholders with a single class of stock and with only individuals, estate and certain trusts eligible as shareholders. Nonresident aliens could not be shareholders.

UNAUTHORIZED ACTS: It is understood that any action taken by the individuals on behalf of the corporation as incorporators are unofficial acts and will remain unofficial acts until the Articles of Incorporation have been filed by the Secretary of State after which a formal Organizational Meeting will be held.

The form opposite is an example of how a typical form for the Preliminary Meeting may be completed.

19. An amount of capital must be stated as to the anticipation of the company's financial needs. The company should always be adequately capitalized. In other words, a company should always have sufficient funds to conduct the operations for which it is incorporated. In this case, the amount of $20,000 has been arbitrarily set forth as the need for capitalization for this particular company.

20. The amount of one million shares is an arbitrary number for the aggregate or total number of shares that the corporation may issue.

21. A dollar amount or "no par" may be inserted as to the amount per share that shall be used as stock value in conjunction with the issuance of stock by the corporation. "No par" simply means that there is not an established dollar amount, even though a set amount of dollars was used for the purchase of the stock. "No par" has been selected.

22. The number of shares in this case has been arbitrarily selected as 1,000,000 in order to allow the company to have adequate growth. The number of shares need not coincide with the amount of par or dollar contribution made for the capitalization of the company.

23. Again "no par" was selected, although a dollar amount per share could have been indicated.

24. The identified shareholder hypothetically indicated that he would invest a specific amount in the company, and this is reflected in the minutes.

25. This amount represents the figure (which again is arbitrary) which the hypothetical investor indicated he would invest.

26. This is the numerical form of the hypothetical investment.

27. This is the second hypothetical individual who indicated an investment interest in the company.

28. This amount represents the figure, which again is arbitrary, as the amount the second hypothetical investor indicated he would invest.

29. This is the numerical form of the hypothetical investment.

30. This is the third hypothetical individual who indicated an investment interest in the company.

31. This amount represents the figure, which again is arbitrary, and which the hypothetical investor indicated he would invest.

32. This is the numerical form of the hypothetical investment.

    NOTE: The three investments of the investors total $20,000 as shown on the preceding page.

33. This figure must be monitored pursuant to the federal tax regulations if the company is to remain a Subchapter S. An attorney should be consulted regarding this, because this figure does change from time to time. This figure of 35 has been arbitrarily set.

Sample Form: Preliminary Meeting of Exetor Company *(continued)*

There being no further business, the meeting was declared adjourned.

Dated at <u>123 Main Street, Chicago, Illinois</u>[34] on this <u>1st</u>[35] day of <u>April</u>[35], <u>1996</u>[35]

_____

<u>ACTING SECRETARY</u>[36]

_____

<u>ACTING PRESIDENT</u>[37]

The form opposite is an example of how a typical form for the Preliminary Meeting may be completed.

34. Arbitrary location.

35. Arbitrary date and year.

36. Signature of Secretary of the corporation.

37. Signature of President of the corporation.

Sample Form
ORGANIZATIONAL MEETING
OF <u>EXETOR COMPANY</u>[1]

The organizational meeting of <u>Exetor Company</u>[1] was called to order on the <u>5th</u>[2] day of <u>April</u>[2], <u>1996</u>[2] at <u>123 Main Street, Chicago, Illinois</u>[3]. Present for the meeting were <u>Elmer Dolby</u>[4], <u>Richard Snull</u>[4], and <u>David Hokey</u>[4], all of whom waived formal notice of the meeting. Also present for the meeting was Attorney <u>Diane J. Alexander</u>[5]. The first order of business was the discussion by the parties relative to the various documents prepared by counsel.

ARTICLES OF INCORPORATION:

The Articles of Incorporation for the new company were reviewed and discussed. The Articles were accepted by the Secretary of State as filed.

BYLAWS:

The Bylaws drafted on behalf of the corporation, reflecting <u>4</u>[6] officers with various duties each, were reviewed by the parties. The Bylaws were approved as read pursuant to the following resolution:

RESOLVED: That the Bylaws drafted for the officers of <u>Exetor Company</u>[7] are hereby adopted as presented.

The foregoing resolution passed unanimously, whereupon the next order of business was a discussion regarding a previous meeting held on the <u>5th</u>[8] day of <u>April</u>[8], <u>1996</u>[8], and a review of said meeting minutes from said meeting.

MEETING MINUTES:

The minutes of the meeting held on the <u>5th</u>[9] day of <u>April</u>[9], <u>1996</u>[9] were reviewed by the parties present and unanimously approved as official acts of the corporation.

<u>TREASURER'S REPORT</u>[10]:

To date, no treasury had been established, therefore, it was unnecessary for a Treasurer's report to be made.

The form opposite is an example of how a typical form for the Organizational Meeting may be completed. A blank version of this form (for your use) appears on pages 121–124.

1. The name of the corporation should be inserted at the very top to identify the company. It should also be inserted as noted in the first line of the preliminary statement for the meeting minutes.

2. The date of the meeting should be noted.

3. The address of the corporation or where the meeting was held should be noted at this juncture.

4. Names of the individuals who attended the meeting should be listed.

5. It is a good practice to often have an attorney present, especially during the course of an organizational meeting, due to legal questions that may arise; therefore, a place for the attorney's identity has been included.

6. The number four (4) is an arbitrary number, and in the particular sample shown, four (4) officers of the corporation were noted.

7. Once again, the name of the corporation should be inserted.

8. The date that the resolution was passed should be noted. Generally, this is the same date as the meeting minutes.

9. Indicates the date when the earlier meeting was held. This format would be followed in all subsequent meetings where the prior meeting would be reflected.

10. In the event revenues have been received by the corporation, the source and reason for the revenues should be stated, along with a statement relative to any expenditures. In other words, a treasury report should be provided.

Sample Form: Organizational Meeting of Exetor Company *(continued)*

BANK ACCOUNT:

It was reported by Elmer Dolby[11] that a bank account would be opened at Last National Bank[12], and the appropriate corporate resolution had been presented for review and adoption by the incorporators.

CAPITALIZATION:

It was decided that the corporation would be capitalized for the sum of Twenty Thousand Dollars ($20,000)[13] or an investment of Ten Thousand Dollars ($10,000)[14] from Elmer Dolby[15], Five Thousand Dollars ($5,000)[16] from Richard Snull[17] and Five Thousand Dollars ($5,000)[18] from David Hokey[19]. With 1,000,000[20] aggregate shares of the corporation, it was determined that 200,000[21] would be initially issued in the amount of no par ($no par)[22] per share. Therefore, a commitment for 100,000[23] shares by Elmer Dolby[24], a commitment for 50,000[25] shares by Richard Snull[26] and a commitment for 50,000[27] shares by David Hokey[28] had been made to the corporation. Since cash would be contributed, full compliance was expected with Section 351 of the Internal Revenue Code and, accordingly, the following resolution was adopted:

> **RESOLVED:** That the Board of Directors is authorized to issue a single class of stock in Exetor Company[29] to each shareholder in the amount of no par ($no par)[30] per share in such amounts in proportion as will be agreed by the Board of Directors and the individual shareholders and, in this case, to be up to 200,000[31] shares which the Board of Directors will accept in full or in part payment thereof, good and sufficient consideration necessary for the business of the corporation all in compliance to Section 351 of the Internal Revenue Code.

The foregoing resolution was passed unanimously, whereupon each of the parties present, namely Elmer Dolby[32], Richard Snull[33] and David Hokey[34] agree to purchase the shares authorized in the following portions:

100,000[35] by Elmer Dolby

50,000[36] by Richard Snull

50,000[37] by David Hokey

A single certificate of stock will be issued in the name of each shareholder. It was also determined that in consideration of the stock would be payment in compliance to Section 351 of the Internal Revenue Code.

The form opposite is an example of how a typical form for the Organizational Meeting may be completed.

11. Either the President or the Treasurer would report on the establishment of the bank account.

12. The name of the bank should be inserted at this location. It should be noted that very often there is a separate resolution which banks prepare for corporations. Such resolution should be acquired from the bank and should be made a part of the minutes as an attachment. The resolution indicates the amount for which individuals will be authorized to issue checks and whether or not several signatures would be required.

13. The dollar amount of the total investment of all investors should be included at this point.

14. The amount to be contributed by the first investor.

15. The identity of the first investor.

16. The dollar amount invested by the second investor.

17. The name of the second investor.

18. The dollar amount by the third investor.

19. The name of the third investor. With additional investors, an additional amount for each investor and the investor's name should also be shown.

20. The total aggregate number of shares which the corporation is authorized to issue is stated. The figure used is arbitrary in this case.

21. The number of shares actually issued is indicated. The figure chosen was arbitrary.

22. The dollar amount per share that is represented by the stock issued should be stated. If there is a "no par," it should be stated as well.

23. The number of shares purchased by the first investor.

24. The name of the first investor.

25. The number of shares purchased by the second investor.

26. The name of the second investor.

27. The number of shares purchased by the third investor.

28. The name of the third investor. (If there are more investors, the number of shares should be indicated, along with the name of the investor.)

29. Again, the name of the corporation.

30. The dollar amount per share. Here "no par" was chosen.

31. The number of shares issued.

32. The name of the first investor.

33. The name of the second investor.

34. The name of the third investor.

35. The number of shares purchased by the first investor.

36. The number of shares purchased by the second investor.

37. The number of shares purchased by the third investor.

Sample Form: Organizational Meeting of Exetor Company *(continued)*

SMALL BUSINESS CORPORATION:

It was also determined that <u>Exetor Company</u>[38] would qualify as a small business corporation. It was the intention to keep the corporation in the range of qualification for the benefits allowed by the Internal Revenue Code, and including the possible election of Subchapter S status. In regard to that intention of keeping the corporation a small business entity and in conjunction with the foregoing, the following resolution passed unanimously.

RESOLVED: That <u>Exetor Company</u>[38] being a duly organized corporation under the laws of the state of Illinois would be authorized to function as a small business corporation. The initial issue of <u>200,000</u>[39] shares of stock would apply pursuant to the following:

a) Of the initial <u>200,000</u>[39] shares, each share shall be issued at the rate of <u>no par ($no par)</u>[40] per share;

b) That the initial issue of no more than <u>200,000</u>[41] shares shall be made for the aggregate capitalization or investment of <u>Twenty Thousand Dollars ($20,000)</u>[42];

c) The initial issue shall be available to all shareholders or prospective shareholders for the purchase of stock in conjunction with the foregoing up to and including the <u>5th</u>[43] day of <u>April</u>[43], <u>1996</u>[43].

d) Only one class of stock shall be issued.

e) The shareholders shall be individuals, estates or certain trusts as permitted by law.

After the foregoing resolution passed unanimously, the form of stock certificate was reviewed by the parties.

STOCK CERTIFICATE:

A review of the proposed stock certificate was made by all parties which unanimously agreed that the stock certificate presented would be the one used by the corporation. The stock certificates shall be in conformity with <u>Illinois law</u>[44].

<u>SUBCHAPTER S STATUS</u>[45]:

The parties reviewed the 941 form for the purpose of Subchapter S election. It was determined that the parties would elect Subchapter S status and intended to sign the election as soon as the articles were received from the Secretary of State.

The form opposite is an example of how a typical form for the Organizational Meeting may be completed.

38. The name of the corporation.

39. The total number of shares that shall be issued at this particular point in time. (Rarely is it the total or the aggregate number of shares which the corporation is authorized to issue.)

40. The dollar amount or "no par" per share.

41. The number of shares that will be issued at this time.

42. The total amount invested at this time.

43. The date by which each of the shareholders may pay his or her funds to the corporation in exchange for the stock. Often, this is a date in the future which allows the investor sufficient time to make the investment.

44. The state law under which the corporation is issuing its stock.

45. This particular sample shows a Subchapter S election. That is not always necessary. Subchapter S is a portion of the Federal Revenue Code through which special delineated procedures allow individual shareholders to treat the corporation in such manner that a direct tax benefit is derived. An attorney or tax accountant should be consulted in this regard. Most small and/or closely held corporations choose the Subchapter S status; however, it is not necessary to do so. If Subchapter S is not selected, this section should be deleted.

Sample Form: Organizational Meeting of Exetor Company *(continued)*

RATIFICATION OF ACTS:

It was discussed that all actions taken on behalf of Exetor Company[46] be reviewed and approved at each meeting by the Board of Directors or, in this case, the shareholders. Such actions undertaken to date by the corporation were so reviewed, and it was determined that all were properly within the scope and best interest of the corporation and should be ratified accordingly. Therefore, the following resolution was adopted.

RESOLVED: That all actions heretofore taken on behalf of the corporation by the officers, Elmer Dolby[47], Richard Snull[48] and David Hokey[49] are hereby ratified as the official acts of the corporation.

ELECTION OF BOARD OF DIRECTORS:

At this point, it was determined that an election of Board of Directors would be held. Elmer Dolby[50] proposed that the incorporators, namely Elmer Dolby[51], Richard Snull[52] and David Hokey[53] all be elected as the initial Board of Directors. There being no further nominations made, the Board of Directors were unanimously elected as Elmer Dolby[51], Richard Snull[52] and David Hokey[53].

ELECTION OF OFFICERS:

After the election of the Board of Directors, a slate of individuals for the officers of the corporation pursuant to the corporate Bylaws was presented. In this regard, the following individuals were elected officers:

_____[54]   _____[55]   _____[56]

PRESIDENT   **VICE PRESIDENT**   **SECRETARY/TREASURER**

Dated at 123 Main Street, Chicago, Illinois[57] on this 5th[58] day of April[58], 1996[58].

_____[56]

ACTING SECRETARY

This is not a substitute for legal advice. An attorney must be consulted.

The form opposite is an example of how a typical form for the Organizational Meeting may be completed.

46. The name of the corporation appears on the Ratification of Acts discussion.

47. The name of the first shareholder.

48. The name of the second shareholder.

49. The name of the third shareholder.

50. One of the shareholders makes a proposal that the incorporators be elected to the Board of Directors.

51. The first shareholder elected to the Board of Directors.

52. The second shareholder elected to the Board of Directors.

53. The third shareholder elected to the Board of Directors.

54. The individual who is acting President or elected President signs.

55. The individual elected or acting as Vice President signs in this space.

56. The individual elected or acting as Secretary and/or Treasurer would sign in this space.

57. The location where the meeting is held.

58. The date of the meeting.

Sample Form
OFFICIAL NOTICE
ANNUAL STOCKHOLDERS' MEETING

In accordance with Article II, Section 4 of the Bylaws of <u>Exetor Company</u>[1], as amended, notice is hereby given to stockholders of record of the Annual Meeting of Stockholders at the following time and place:

DATE: <u>April 5, 1996</u>[2]

TIME: <u>5:00 pm</u>[3]

LOCATION: <u>123 Main Street, Chicago, Illinois</u>[4]

I certify this to be the official notification of the Annual Meeting of Stockholders of <u>Exetor Company</u>[5] and this notice was delivered in accordance with the Bylaws.

_____ [6] <u>April 5, 1996</u>[7]
President/Secretary   Date

The form opposite is an example of how a typical form for the Official Notice of Annual Stockholders' Meeting form may be completed. A blank version of this form (for your use) appears on page 125.

1. The identity of the corporation.

2. The date of the meeting.

3. The time the meeting is to be held.

4. The location where the meeting is to be held.

5. The name of the corporation again.

6. The signature of the President and/or Secretary.

7. The date on which the notice is sent to the shareholders.

Sample Form
MEETING WAIVER

The undersigned hereby states that notice of a meeting of the Board of Directors of Exetor Company[1] was provided to me on the 15th[2] day of February[2], 1996[2], for a meeting which was to occur on the 1st[3] day of April[3], 1996[3], and I hereby waive formal notice of said meeting and hereby authorize the corporation's Board of Directors to act on my behalf in my absence.

STATE OF ILLINOIS [4]
COUNTY OF COOK [4]

_____ [5]

SHAREHOLDER

Subscribed and sworn to before a Notary Public on this 15th[6] day of February[6], 1996[6].

_____ [7]

NOTARY PUBLIC, STATE OF ILLINOIS[8]

The form opposite is an example of how a typical form for a Meeting Waiver may be completed. A blank version of this form (for your use) appears on page 127.

1. The name of the corporation.

2. The date on which the meeting waiver was provided.

3. The date on which the meeting was to occur.

4. The identity of the state and county.

5. The signature of the shareholder waiving a notice of the meeting.

6. The date on which the shareholder signed the document.

7. The signature of the Notary Public.

8. The identity of the state.

Sample Form
FIRST BOARD OF DIRECTORS' MEETING
OF <u>EXETOR COMPANY</u>[1]
(Name of Corporation)

The first meeting of the Board of Directors of <u>Exetor Company</u>[1] was called to order at <u>123 Main Street, Chicago, Illinois</u>[2] on the <u>5th</u>[3] day of <u>April</u>[3], <u>1996</u>[3]. Present for the meeting were <u>Elmer Dolby</u>[4], <u>Richard Snull</u>[5], and <u>David Hokey</u>[6], each of whom waived formal notice of said meeting.

MEETING MINUTES:

The meeting minutes of the Preliminary Meeting held on the <u>5th</u>[7] day of <u>February</u>[7], <u>1996</u>[7], and the meeting minutes of the Organizational Meeting on the <u>5th</u>[8] day of <u>March</u>[8], <u>1996</u>[8], were read and approved with changes.

<u>TREASURER'S REPORT</u>[9]:

The Treasurer's report was deferred until the next meeting due to the fact that arrangements were being made to open appropriate bank accounts and assemble the funds for the investment by the respective shareholders.

OFFICIAL BUSINESS:

It was anticipated that the first corporate account would be developed sometime within the next 30 days; an appropriate contract would be prepared and signed at that time.

STOCK ISSUE:

It was determined that <u>Exetor Company</u>[10] would qualify as a small business corporation and it was the intention to keep the corporation in the range of qualification for benefits allowed under the Internal Revenue Code including being the election of Subchapter S which was decided to be undertaken in the meeting of the general shareholders held on the <u>15th</u>[11] day of <u>February</u>[11], <u>1996</u>[11]. In regard with the intent of keeping the corporation a small business entity and in conjunction with the foregoing, the following resolution passed unanimously:

The form opposite is an example of how a typical form for the First Board of Directors' Meeting may be completed. A blank version of this form (for your use) appears on pages 129–131.

1. The name of the corporation.

2. The location where the meeting was held.

3. The date the meeting was held.

4. The identity of the first shareholder present.

5. The identity of the second shareholder present.

6. The identity of the third shareholder present.

7. The date of the prior meeting, in this case, the Preliminary Meeting.

8. The date the Organizational Meeting was held.

9. If funds have been received and expenditures made, a full Treasurer's report should either appear here or be attached as an appendix.

10. The name of the corporation.

11. The date the meeting of the general shareholders was held.

Sample Form: First Board of Directors' Meeting of Exetor Company *(continued)*

RESOLVED: That Exetor Company[12], being a duly organized corporation under the laws of the State of Illinois[13], should be authorized to function as a small business corporation and the initial issue of 200,000[14] shares of stock would apply pursuant to the following:

A. Of the initial 200,000[14] shares, each share shall be issued at the rate of no par ($no par)[15] per share.

B. That, in the initial issue, no more than 200,000[16] shares shall be authorized for an aggregate capitalization or investment of $20,000[17].

C. The initial issue shall be available to all shareholders or prospective shareholders for the purchase of stock in conjunction with the foregoing, up to and including the 1st[18] day of June[18], 1996[18].

D. Only a single class of stock shall be issued.[19]

E. The shareholders shall be individuals, estates and/or certain trusts as permitted by law.

After the foregoing resolution passed unanimously, it was decided that the stock certificates would be issued, however, would be held until each investor had invested his complete amount of interest.

FEDERAL I.D. NUMBER:

It was necessary for the corporation to complete its Federal I.D. Application (Form No. 2553)[20], which was completed for filing.

SUBCHAPTER S STATUS:

It was decided that the corporation engage as a Subchapter S; therefore, a Form No. 941 would be completed by the shareholders. All parties agreed that this was the best course for the corporation to follow.

ELECTION OF OFFICERS:

A slate of officers was proposed, and the following individuals were elected as officers of the corporation:

Elmer Dolby	President[21]
Richard Snull	Vice President[22]
David Hokey	Secretary[23]
David Hokey	Treasurer[24]

The form opposite is an example of how a typical form for the First Board of Directors' Meeting may be completed.

12. The name of the corporation.

13. The state in which the corporation exists and under whose laws it is governed.

14. The number of shares to be issued. This amount should be consistent with the amount shown in the Organizational Meeting. The figure of 200,000 was selected arbitrarily.

15. The dollar amount or "no par" per share. This should also be consistent with the amount shown in the Organizational Meeting.

16. Number of shares to be issued initially. The 200,000 figure was used arbitrarily.

17. The dollar amount of the total contribution or investment by the shareholders to be made at this time. The $20,000 figure is arbitrary.

18. The date by which the shareholders must make their investment. Generally, this is a date in the future allowing the shareholders to make an investment up to and including the date shown. (No other resolution such as this resolution may be issued prior to the fulfillment of the stock investment and prior to the conclusion of this date.)

19. The class of the stock or the series of the stock should be indicated at this point.

20. The 2553 Form is the form which allows for an application to the Internal Revenue Service for a Federal I.D. number.

21. The name of the elected President.

22. The name of the elected Vice President.

23. The name of the elected Secretary.

24. The name of the elected Treasurer.

Sample Form: First Board of Directors' Meeting of Exetor Company *(continued)*

NEW BUSINESS:

No new business was discussed at this time.

AMENDMENTS:

No amendments were found to be necessary to the corporation Bylaws.

RATIFICATION OF ACTS:

In conjunction with the parties of the corporation and pursuant to each of the incorporators and officers acting on behalf of the corporation, the following resolution was adopted:

RESOLVED: That all actions heretofore undertaken by each of the officers on behalf of the corporation are hereby authorized as full and complete acts of the corporation; and that the corporation shall indemnify each of the principals, incorporators and shareholders as well as officers for said acts.

The foregoing resolution was passed unanimously. There being no further business, the meeting was declared adjourned.

Dated at <u>123 Main Street, Chicago, Illinois</u>[25], on this <u>5th</u>[26] day of <u>April</u>[26], <u>1996</u>[26].

_____[27]

SECRETARY

**The form opposite is an example of how a typical form for the First Board of Directors'
Meeting may be completed.**

25. The location where the meeting was held.

26. The date when the meeting occurred.

27. The signature of the secretary.

Sample Form
PROXY

I, <u>Richard Snull</u>[1], being a shareholder of <u>Exetor Company</u>[2], do hereby acknowl-edge receipt of the following items to be discussed at the company annual meeting on <u>April 5, 1996</u>[3]:

1. <u>Notice of the Annual Meeting</u>[4];
2. <u>The stated special purpose of the meeting contained in the notice</u>[5];
3. <u>A slate of proposed officers</u>[6];
4. <u>This Proxy</u>[7].

In conjunction with the accepted business practices which govern annual meet-ings under <u>Illinois law</u>[8], I state that I understand the stated purpose of the annual meeting as set forth in the enclosed notice and do hereby provide to <u>Elmer Dolby</u>[9], President of the <u>Exetor Company</u>[10], my proxy to vote my <u>5,000</u>[11] shares as he deems fit and necessary so long as such vote relates to the enclosed documents.

_____[12]

SHAREHOLDER'S NAME

Subscribed and sworn to before the undersigned Notary Public of <u>Cook</u>[13] County of the State of <u>Illinois</u>[14].

_____[15]

NOTARY PUBLIC, STATE OF <u>ILLINOIS</u>[16]

The form opposite is an example of how a typical Proxy form may be completed. A blank version of this form (for your use) appears on page 133.

1. Name of the shareholder should be presented.

2. The name of the company.

3. The date the annual meeting is to occur.

4. Generally, a notice accompanies the proxy.

5. Generally, a specific purpose of the meeting, in addition to it being an annual meeting, will be stated and provided to the shareholder.

6. Very often a slate of proposed officers or directors is presented.

7. The proxy itself is presented to the shareholder.

8. This particular proxy is drafted with the expectation to comply with Illinois law.

9. The identity of the President or some other officer who is given the proxy appears at this juncture.

10. The name of the company.

11. The number of shares owned by the particular shareholder.

12. The signature of the shareholder.

13. The county in which the shareholder signs the proxy.

14. The state in which the shareholder signs the proxy.

15. The signature of the Notary Public.

16. The state in which the shareholder signs the proxy.

Sample Form
REGISTERED AGENT'S STATEMENT
OF RESIGNATION TO THE <u>SECRETARY OF STATE</u>[1]
FOR THE STATE OF <u>ILLINOIS</u>[2]:

<u>Pursuant to the Illinois Business Corporation Act of 1983</u>[3], the undersigned registered agent states:

1. The name of the registered agent is <u>Elmer Dolby</u>[4].

2. The registered agent resigns the appointment as registered agent for the following corporation: <u>Exetor Company</u>[5].

3. [optional] <u>Upon the effective date of the resignation, the registered office is also discontinued</u>[6].

The effective date and time of this document is:

<u>April 5, 1996</u> [date][7]

<u>4:00 pm</u> [time][8]

_____[9]

NAME OF REGISTERED AGENT

_____[10]

[signature]

REGISTERED AGENT

Subscribed and sworn to before a Notary Public on the <u>5th</u>[11] day of <u>April</u>[11], <u>1996</u>[11].

_____[12]

NOTARY PUBLIC

This is not a substitute for legal advice. An attorney must be consulted.

The form opposite is an example of how a typical form for the Registered Agent's Statement of Resignation may be completed. A blank version of this form (for your use) appears on page 135.

1. The identity of the appropriate government authority is inserted here. In this case, it is the Secretary of State.

2. The proper state must be identified. In this case, it is Illinois.

3. The Illinois Business Corporation Act is identified as the act under which this particular registered agent change is occurring.

4. The name of the existing registered agent must be indicated.

5. The name of the corporation from which the registered agent is resigning.

6. This item is optional. Upon the resignation, the registered office may be discontinued if the office is to be changed. This should be specifically stated. Normally, a new registered agent and a new registered office should be indicated.

7. The effective date of the resignation.

8. The effective time of the resignation.

9. The name of the registered agent.

10. The signature of the registered agent.

11. The date signed by the registered agent before the Notary Public.

12. The signature of the Notary Public.

Sample Form:
STOCK CERTIFICATE

NUMBER   **SHARES**

2[1]   5,000[2]

(NAME OF COMPANY)   EXETOR COMPANY[3]

(ADDRESS)   123 MAIN STREET, CHICAGO, ILLINOIS[4]

THIS CERTIFIES THAT Richard Snull[5] *is the owner of* 5,000[6] *shares of* no par[7] *each of the Capital Stock of* Exetor Company[8] *transferable only on the books of the Corporation by the holder hereof in person or by Attorney upon surrender of this Certificate properly endorsed. This Corporation is organized under the Laws of the State of* Illinois[9] *and pursuant to the* Illinois Business Corporation Act[10].

IN WITNESS WHEREOF, *the said Corporation has caused this Certificate to be signed by its duly authorized officers and to be sealed with the Seal of the Corporation this* 5th[11] *day of* April[11] *A.D.* 1996[11].

SHARES (no par) EACH[12]

_____ [13]   _____ [14]

SECRETARY OF CORPORATION   PRESIDENT OF CORPORATION

The form opposite is an example of how a typical Stock Certificate form may be completed. A blank version of this form (for your use) appears on page 137.

1. The identity of the stock certificate number.

2. The number of shares issued with this stock certificate.

3. The name of the company.

4. The address of the company.

5. The name of the shareholder who is receiving the stock.

6. The number of shares which the stockholder has acquired.

7. The price of the stock or "no par" value of the stock.

8. The name of the corporation.

9. The state where the stock certificates are issued.

10. The state laws under which the corporation is authorized to issue stock.

11. The date the stock certificate is issued.

12. The value of the stock certificate or the "no par" value to be indicated.

13. The signature of the Secretary of the corporation.

14. The signature of the President of the corporation.

Sample Form
AGREEMENT TO RESTRICT TRANSFER OF STOCK
<u>EXETOR COMPANY</u>[1]
(NAME OF COMPANY)

AGREEMENT made this <u>5th</u>[2] day of <u>April</u>[2], <u>1996</u>[2], among <u>Exetor Company</u>[3], an <u>Illinois</u>[4] Corporation, with its principal office at <u>123 Main Street, Chicago, Illinois</u>[5] (address) and the following individuals (collectively referred to as "stockholders"):

<u>Elmer Dolby</u>[6]

<u>Richard Snull</u>[7]

<u>David Hokey</u> [8]

Whereas, the stockholders are the holders of record and beneficial owners of all shares of the issued and outstanding stock of the only issued class of stock of <u>Exetor Company</u>[9] an <u>Illinois</u>[10] Corporation, with its principal office <u>123 Main Street, Chicago, Illinois</u>[11] and;

Whereas, Corporation is an "S" Corporation as defined in Section 1361(a)(1) of the Internal Revenue Code of 1986, having filed an election to be an "S" Corporation on the <u>5th</u>[12] day of <u>April</u>[12], <u>1996</u>[12], which was effective as of the first day of its taxable year that began <u>April 15, 1996</u>[13].

Whereas, the parties desire to continue Corporation "S" election in effect until such time, if any, as the selection is terminated by revocation by Corporation with the consent of the majority of the shares of Corporation's issued and outstanding stock.

Whereas, it is the desire of the parties to restrict the transfer of stock.

Now, therefore, the parties agree as follows:

1. **TERM OF THE AGREEMENT:** The term of this agreement shall be from and including the <u>5th</u>[14] day of <u>April</u>[14], <u>1996</u>[14], through and including the day before the first day that Corporation is no longer an "S" Corporation.

2. **DEFINITION OF TRANSFER:** As used in this agreement, the term "transfer" means any sale, exchange, gift, bequest, or any other beneficial ownership of shares of Corporation's stock including, without limitation, a transaction that creates any form of joint ownership in the stock between transferor and one or more persons (whether or not that other person is the spouse of the transferor).

The form opposite is an example of how a typical form for the Agreement to Restrict Transfer of Stock may be completed. A blank version of this form (for your use) appears on pages 139–145.

1. The name of the company.

2. The date the agreement is signed.

3. The name of the company or corporation.

4. The state in which the corporation is organized.

5. The location of the principal office, generally, the registered office of the corporation.

6. The name of the first shareholder.

7. The name of the second shareholder.

8. The name of the third shareholder.

9. The name of the corporation.

10. The state in which the corporation or company is organized.

11. The address of the principal office.

12. The date on which a Subchapter S election occurred.

13. The date the taxable year began.

14. The date from which the agreement commences.

Sample Form: Agreement to Restrict Transfer of Stock of Exetor Company *(continued)*

3. **PERMITTED INTERVIVOS TRANSFERS WITHOUT CONSENT OF OTHER SHAREHOLDERS:** The following transfers of stock may be made by a stockholder during his lifetime without the consent of all or any of the other stockholders of the Corporation.

a. **Transfer to Spouse or Children of Stockholder with No Net Increase in the Number of Corporation's Stockholders:** A stockholder may transfer any or all of his shares to his spouse or any one of his children provided that immediately after the transfer, the number of Corporation's stockholders is unchanged from prior to the transfer, as counted by the applicable provisions of the Internal Revenue Code, and the transferee meets all requirements to qualify as an "S" Corporation stockholder.

b. **Transfer to Voting Trust:** A stockholder may transfer all or any part of his shares of stock in a Corporation to a voting trust provided that after the transfer, that stockholder remains the beneficial owner of all of the transferred shares.

c. **Transfers to Grantor Trust:** A stockholder may transfer all or any part of his shares of stock in Corporation to a trust ("grantor trust") provided the following conditions are met:

(i) At all times from the date shares of Corporation's stock are first transferred to the grantor trust through the earlier of the date of the grantor's death or the termination of the trust, the grantor must be treated under the provisions of Subpart E of Part I of Subchapter 1 of Subtitle A of the Internal Revenue Code as in effect on the date of the transfer, as the owner of the trust.

(ii) If the grantor trust is to continue for the grantor's life, then on the death of the grantor, the trust must terminate and all shares of Corporation's stock held by the trust must be distributed in accordance with Paragraph 6.

(iii) If the grantor trust can terminate before the death of the grantor, the trust agreement must provide that on the termination of the trust, all shares of Corporation's stock must be distributed to the grantor.

4. **TRANSFERS PERMITTED AFTER STOCK IS OFFERED TO CORPORATION OR OTHER SHAREHOLDERS:** A stockholder shall not, during his lifetime, transfer or dispose of any portion or all of his stock interest in the Corporation other than as provided for in Paragraph 3, unless he shall first offer in writing such stock to Corporation at a purchase price to be established annually by a majority vote of the Board of Directors. If the stock is not purchased by the Corporation within 90 days of the receipt of the offer, then the stock not so purchased shall be offered for sale at same price and shall be subject to an option on the part of each of the shareholders to purchase, at a minimum, the number of shares proportionate to their current stockholding in the Corporation. The option to

The form opposite is an example of how a typical form for the Agreement to Restrict Transfer of Stock may be completed.

No information needs to be added to this particular page of the form.

Sample Form: Agreement to Restrict Transfer of Stock of Exetor Company *(continued)*

purchase stock by the other shareholders must be exercised within 30 days from the time such option became available to the shareholders. If all of the stock of the stockholder desiring to make a disposition thereof is not purchased by the Corporation or other shareholders within 120 days after same is offered for such sale, the selling stockholder shall have the option of selling or transferring his stock in the Corporation to any other as follows, provided that the stock is not sold or transferred at a price less than was offered to the Corporation or other stockholders:

a. **Transfer of all Shares to United States Citizen:** Any stockholder may transfer all, but not less than all, of his shares to an individual who is a citizen of the United States at the time the transfer is made provided that the transferer retains no interest in those shares (whether as a joint tenant owner, beneficiary, trustee, creditor, or otherwise) after the transfer.

b. **Transfer of Some of Shares to United States Citizen:** Any stockholder may transfer less than all of his shares to an individual who is a citizen of the United States at the time the transfer is made, provided that the majority of Corporation's shareholders approve of the transaction and that, immediately after the transfer, the number of the Corporation's stockholders does not exceed the maximum number an "S" Corporation is allowed to have under the applicable provisions of the Internal Revenue Code, as then in effect.

c. **Transfers to Trust Owned by Individual Other Than Grantor:** A stockholder may transfer all or any part of his shares of stock in the Corporation to a trust ("beneficiary trust") provided that the following conditions are met:

(i) One individual ("beneficiary") who is a citizen of the United States, must be treated under the provisions of Subpart E of Part I of Subchapter J of Chapter 1 of Subtitle A of the Internal Revenue Code as in effect on the date of the transfer, as the owner of all of the trust at all times from the date shares of the Corporation's stock are first transferred to the trust through the earlier of the date of the beneficiary's death or the date of the termination of the trust.

(ii) If less than all of a stockholder's shares of Corporation's stock are transferred to the beneficiary trust, and if the beneficiary is not already a stockholder in the Corporation at the time of the transfer, then provided that the majority of the Corporation's shareholders approve of the transaction and that, immediately after the transfer, the number of the Corporation's stockholders does not exceed the maximum number a Sub-S Corporation is allowed to have under the applicable provisions of the Internal Revenue Code, as then in effect.

The form opposite is an example of how a typical form for the Agreement to Restrict Transfer of Stock may be completed.

No information needs to be added to this particular page of the form.

Sample Form: Agreement to Restrict Transfer of Stock of Exetor Company *(continued)*

(iii) If the beneficiary trust is to continue for the beneficiary's life, the trust agreement must provide that, on the death of the beneficiary, the trust must terminate and all the shares of the Corporation's stock held by the trust must be distributed to one individual who is a citizen of the United States.

(iv) If the beneficiary trust can terminate before the death of the beneficiary, the trust agreement must provide that on the termination of the trust, all shares of the Corporation's stock must be distributed to the beneficiary.

5. **PERMITTED INTERVIVOS TRANSFERS WITH CONSENT OF OTHER STOCK-HOLDERS:** A stockholder may make a transfer not described in Paragraph 3 or Paragraph 4 of this agreement of all or any of his shares of stock in the Corporation to any person who, under the applicable provisions of the Internal Revenue Code in effect at the time of the transfer, is eligible to be stockholder in an "S" Corporation, provided all of the following conditions are met:

a. Immediately after the transfer, the number of Corporation's stockholders does not exceed the maximum number an "S" Corporation is allowed to have under the applicable provisions of the Internal Revenue Code, as then in effect.

b. All persons who are stockholders in the Corporation at the time of the transfer must consent in writing to the transfer.

6. **TRANSFER BY WILL OR BY OPERATION OF LAW AT DECEDENT'S DEATH:** Transfer of stock due to the death and/or pursuant to the Last Will and Testament of any shareholders must satisfy the requirement of Paragraphs 3, 4 or 5 of this agreement.

7. **TRANSFERS TO INELIGIBLE PERSONS:** Each stockholder agrees to not transfer, or attempt to transfer, any shares of stock in the Corporation now owned by that stockholder, or hereafter acquired by that stockholder, to a person who is not eligible to be a stockholder of an "S" Corporation under the provisions of the Internal Revenue Code as in effect at the time of the transfer.

8. **TRANSFER OF SHARES IN VIOLATION OF AGREEMENT NULL AND VOID:** Any purported transfer of shares of Corporation's stock made in violation of the provisions of this agreement shall be null and void and the purported transfer shall be declared voidable.

9. **GRANT OF OPTION:** A stockholder may not grant, sell, give or, in any way, create in any person any option, warrant or other right (including any "option" to acquire all or any part of that shareholder's shares of Corporation's stock) if that person is not eligible to be a stockholder in an "S" Corporation at the time of the grant, etc. A shareholder may not grant, sell, give or, in any way, create in any person who is eligible to be a shareholder

The form opposite is an example of how a typical form for the Agreement to Restrict Transfer of Stock may be completed.

No information needs to be added to this particular page of the form.

Sample Form: Agreement to Restrict Transfer of Stock of Exetor Company *(continued)*

in an "S" Corporation any option to acquire all or any part of that shareholder's shares of Corporation's stock unless the following requirements are met:

a. The option must be in writing.

b. The option must specifically provide that the exercise of the right to acquire stock will be treated as a transfer for purposes of this agreement and that the option may not be exercised if:

(i) The holder, at the time of the proposed exercise, is not eligible to be a shareholder of an "S" Corporation even if the holder was eligible at the time they obtained the option, or;

(ii) Immediately after the exercise of the option, the number of Corporation's stockholders would exceed the maximum number an "S" Corporation is allowed to have under the applicable provisions of the Internal Revenue Code, as then in effect. In the event of change in the Internal Revenue Code, this agreement should be modified to appropriately conform in order to maintain the "S" Corporation status.

c. All persons who are stockholders in the Corporation at the time of the grant, etc. of the option must consent in writing to the grant, etc.

Any purported grant, etc., of an option to a person not eligible to be a stockholder in an "S" Corporation or to an eligible person in violation of any of the above requirements shall be null and void. Any purported exercise of an option purported to be granted whose grant is null and void shall be null and void and shall be ineffective to create any interest in the purported grantee in any shares of Corporation's stock. Any purported exercise of an option validly granted shall be null and void if that exercise would create any interest in shares of Corporation's stock in a person not eligible to be a stockholder in an "S" Corporation.

10. **PLEDGE OF STOCK:** A stockholder may not pledge, hypothecate, or otherwise create a security interest in all or part of that stockholder's shares of stock in the Corporation without first obtaining the consent, in writing, of all persons who are stockholders in the Corporation at the time of the proposed pledge, etc.

11. **ENDORSEMENT ON STOCK CERTIFICATE:** There shall be legibly stamped on each stock certificate issued by the Corporation during the time this agreement is in effect the following statement:

"None of the shares of stock represented by this certificate may be transferred, no interest in all or any of those shares (whether as owner, creditor or otherwise) may be created, and no right to acquire all or any of those shares may be obtained, except in

The form opposite is an example of how a typical form for the Agreement to Restrict Transfer of Stock may be completed.

No information needs to be added to this particular page of the form.

Sample Form: Agreement to Restrict Transfer of Stock of Exetor Company *(continued)*

compliance with the terms of the Stock Transfer Agreement dated the 5th[15] day of April[15], 1996[15], among Exetor Company[16] and its then stockholders. A copy of that agreement is on file in the office of the Secretary of the Corporation. Any interest created in any of the shares represented by this certificate in violation of the terms of that agreement shall be null and void.

12. **TRANSFERS BOUND BY AGREEMENT:** Notwithstanding anything else contained in this agreement, no transfer of shares during the term of this agreement shall be effective to vest any right, title or ownership, in the transferee unless the transferee agrees, in writing, in an instrument filed with the Secretary of the Corporation, to be bound by all the provisions of this agreement. Without limiting the foregoing, a transferee, by accepting any transferred shares, shall be deemed to have become a party to this agreement with respect to those transferred shares to the same extent as if that transferee had executed this agreement.

13. **INDEMNIFICATION FOR BREACH:** If any stockholder breaches any term of this agreement in a manner that causes the Corporation's Subchapter "S" election to terminate, that stockholder ("indemnitor") shall indemnify each of the other stockholders ("indemnitees") for the amount of that stockholder's share of lost Federal Income Tax benefits resulting from the termination during the period the Corporation is ineligible to make a Subchapter "S" election under the applicable provisions of the Internal Revenue Code.

a. Definition of Federal Income Tax Benefits: For purposes of this Paragraph 13, a stockholder's share of Federal Income Tax benefits equals the excess of:

(i) The stockholder's pro rata share of Federal Income Taxes imposed on the Corporation as a "C" Corporation plus the stockholder's Federal Income Tax on dividend distributions by the Corporation, over

(ii) The stockholder's pro rata share of Federal Income Taxes that would have been imposed on the Corporation as an "S" Corporation if it had the same items of income, loss, deduction and credit that has a "C" Corporation, plus the amount of Federal Income Taxes that the stockholder would have paid on the items of income, etc., that would have been passed through to the stockholder if it were an "S" Corporation. The Corporation and the stockholders shall make reasonable efforts to mitigate the loss of Federal Income Tax benefits resulting from the termination by seeking to have the termination treated as inadvertent under Section 1352(f) of the Internal Revenue Code. If the termination is not treated as inadvertent, the Corporation and the stockholders shall seek the Secretary of the Treasury's consent to a new election as soon as possible.

The form opposite is an example of how a typical form for the Agreement to Restrict Transfer of Stock may be completed.

15. The date of the Stock Transfer Agreement.

16. The name of the company.

Sample Form: Agreement to Restrict Transfer of Stock of Exetor Company *(continued)*

14. **BENEFIT:** This agreement shall be binding upon and shall insure to the benefit of the parties to this agreement, and their respective heirs, executors, administrators, legal representatives, and assignees.

15. **APPLICABLE LAW:** This agreement shall be governed by, and interpreted and construed under and in accordance with, the laws of the State of <u>Illinois</u>[17].

16. **MODIFICATION:** No modification, rescission, cancellation, amendment or termination of this agreement shall be effective unless it is in writing and is signed by all parties to the agreement. In the event of change in the Internal Revenue Code, this agreement shall be modified to appropriately conform to preserve its "S" Corporation status.

17. **COUNTERPARTS:** This agreement may be executed in two or more counterparts, each of which shall be deemed an original and all of which, taken together, shall constitute one agreement.

18. **NOTIFICATION OF TRANSFER:** The Corporation must be given written notice not less than 30 days prior to any proposed transfer of stock ownership. Such written notification must include sufficient information to insure that the terms of this agreement will be met by the proposed transfer.

In witness whereof, the parties have executed this agreement:

<u>Elmer Dolby</u>[18a]   _____ [18b]
Name of Shareholder   Signature of Shareholder

<u>Richard Snull</u>[19a]   _____ [19b]
Name of Shareholder   Signature of Shareholder

<u>David Hokey</u>[20a]   _____ [20b]
Name of Shareholder   Signature of Shareholder

Approved on behalf of <u>Exetor Company</u>[21] by:

_____ [22]   _____ [23]

PRESIDENT   **SECRETARY**

This is not a substitute for legal advice. An attorney must be consulted.

Copyright © 1996 LAW ✓™

The form opposite is an example of how a typical form for the Agreement To Restrict Transfer of Stock may be completed.

17. The state in which the company or corporation was organized.

18a. Name of the first shareholder.

18b. Signature of the first shareholder.

19a. Name of the second shareholder.

19b. Signature of the second shareholder.

20a. Name of the third shareholder.

20b. Signature of the third shareholder.

21. Name of the company.

22. Signature of the President of the company.

23. Signature of the Secretary of the company.

Sample Form
STOCK REGISTER

Certificate Number	Date of Issue	Shareholder's Name	Address	Shares in Certificate
1	4/5/96	Elmer Dolby	123 Main Street Chicago, IL	100,000[1]
2	4/5/96	Richard Snull	333 High Cliff Dr. Chicago, IL	50,000[2]
3	4/5/96	David Hokey	987 Swimmer Lane Chicago, IL	50,000[3]

The form opposite is an example of how a typical Stock Register form may be completed. A blank version of this form (for your use) appears on page 147.

1. The first certificate that is issued, the date the certificate was issued, the shareholder's name, the address of the shareholder, and the number of shares in the certificate issued.

2. The identity of the second stock certificate, the date it was issued, the shareholder's name, the address of the shareholder, and the number of shares in that certificate.

3. The number of the third certificate issued, the date it was issued, the shareholder's name, the address of that shareholder, plus the number of shares in that certificate.

CHAPTER • 5

Blank Forms

The forms in this chapter are blank versions of the completed forms in chapter 4; these forms are for your use.

Form One

_____ OF INCORPORATION
OF _____

TO THE _____
OF THE STATE OF _____

The undersigned persons, acting as incorporators of a corporation organized pursuant to the _____, as amended, hereby adopt the following Articles of Incorporation.

ARTICLE I

NAME: The name of the corporation under Chapter_____ shall be known as: _____.

ARTICLE II

PERIOD OF DURATION: The period of duration of _____ shall be perpetual unless dissolved under the laws of the State of _____ or changed in accordance with these Articles and the corporation Bylaws.

ARTICLE III

PURPOSE: This corporation is organized for the purpose of conducting proper aspects of business in a manner in which the corporation was organized for operation under Chapter _____ of the State of _____ as amended, with the principal purpose of _____
_____.

ARTICLE IV

AGGREGATE SHARES: The aggregate number of shares which the corporation is authorized to issue is _____, consisting of one class with _____ par value. The voting rights will be exercised in direct relation to the number of shares held by the single class established.

ARTICLE V

REGISTERED OFFICE/AGENT: The address of the initial office of the corporation shall be _____,_____. The name of its initial registered agent at said address is _____ pursuant to Section _____.

ARTICLE VI

BOARD OF DIRECTORS: The number of directors constituting the initial Board of Directors will be _____ and each shall serve as director until his successor is elected and qualifies under the Bylaws of the corporation. After the initial Board of Directors, the Board shall consist of such number of directors as shall be fixed and/or determined by the shareholders from time to time at each annual meeting thereof, at which time the directors are to be elected. The initial directors of the new corporation shall be the undersigned incorporators.

ARTICLE VII

BYLAWS: The Bylaws of _____ may contain any restrictions on the transfer of the shares of stock of the corporation as well as the issuance of any bonds or notes.

ARTICLE VIII

CORPORATE EXISTENCE: The corporation's existence shall begin on the day these _____ are filed with the _____ and recorded at the office of the _____ County Recorder.

ARTICLE IX

INCORPORATORS: The names and addresses of the incorporators are:

_____   /s/_____
_____
_____

_____   /s/_____
_____
_____

_____   /s/_____
_____
_____

STATE OF _____)

)ss

COUNTY OF _____)

On this _____ day of _____, 19___, before me, the undersigned Notary Public, personally appeared _____, _____ and _____ to me known to be the persons named in and who executed the foregoing Articles of Incorporation and they acknowledged that they executed the same as their voluntary act and deed.

_____

NOTARY PUBLIC

This is not a substitute for legal advice. An attorney must be consulted.

Form Two

BYLAWS (4 OFFICERS)
OF _____

ARTICLE I. PRINCIPAL OFFICE

The principal office of the corporation in the State of _____ shall be located in the City of _____, County of _____. The corporation may have such other offices, either within or without the State of _____, as the Board of Directors may designate or as the business of the corporation may require from time to time (pursuant to _____).

ARTICLE II. SHAREHOLDERS

SECTION I. ANNUAL MEETING. The annual meeting of the shareholders shall be held in the last week of _____ of each year, beginning in 19___ for the purpose of electing Directors and for the transaction of such other business as may come before the meeting. If the day fixed for the annual meeting shall be a legal holiday in the State of _____, such meeting shall be held on the next succeeding business day. If the election of Directors shall not be held on the day designated herein for any annual meeting of the shareholders, or any adjournment thereof, the Board of Directors shall cause the election to be held at a special meeting of the shareholders as soon thereafter as conveniently possible (pursuant to _____).

SECTION 2. SPECIAL MEETINGS. Special meetings of the shareholders, for any purpose or purposes, unless otherwise prescribed by statute, may be called by the President or by the Board of Directors, and shall be called by the President at the request of two shareholders (pursuant to _____).

SECTION 3. PLACE OF MEETING. The Board of Directors may designate any place, either within or without the State of _____, as the place of meeting for any annual meeting or for any special meeting called by the Board of Directors. A waiver of notice signed by all shareholders entitled to vote at a meeting may designate any place, either within or without the State of _____, unless otherwise prescribed by statute, as the place for the holding of such meeting. If no designation is made, or if a special meeting is otherwise called, the place of meeting shall be the principal office of the corporation in the State of _____.

SECTION 4. NOTICE OF MEETING. Written notice stating the place, day and hour of the meeting and, in case of special meeting, the purpose or purposes for which the meeting is called, unless otherwise prescribed by statute, shall be delivered not less than _____ nor more than _____ days before the date of the meeting, either personally or by mail, by or at the direction of the _____, or the _____, or the persons calling the meeting, to each shareholder of record entitled to vote at such meeting. If mailed, such notice shall be deemed to be delivered when deposited in the United States mail, addressed to the shareholder at his address as it appears on the stock transfer books of the corporation, with postage thereon prepaid (pursuant to _____).

SECTION 5. QUORUM. A majority of the outstanding shares of the corporation entitled to vote, represented in person or by proxy, shall constitute a quorum at a meeting of shareholders. If less than the outstanding shares are represented at a meeting, a majority of the shares so represented may adjourn the meeting from time to time without further notice. At such adjourned meeting at which a quorum shall be present or represented, any business may be transacted which might have been transacted at the meeting as originally noticed. The shareholders present at a duly organized meeting may continue to transact business until adjournment, notwithstanding the withdrawal of enough shareholders to leave less than a quorum (pursuant to _____).

SECTION 6. PROXIES. At all meetings of shareholders, a shareholder may vote in person or by proxy executed in writing by the shareholder or by his duly authorized attorney in fact. Such proxy shall be filed with the _____ of the corporation before or at the time of the meeting. No proxy shall be valid after four weeks from the date of its execution, unless otherwise provided in the proxy (pursuant to _____).

SECTION 7. VOTING OF SHARES. Subject to the provisions of any language to the contrary of this Article II, each outstanding share entitled to vote shall be entitled to one vote upon each matter submitted to a vote at the meeting of the shareholders (pursuant to _____).

SECTION 8. CUMULATIVE VOTING. Unless otherwise provided by law, at each election for Directors, every shareholder entitled to vote at such election shall have the right to vote, in person or by proxy, the number of shares owned by him for as many persons as there are Directors to be elected and for whose election he has a right to vote, or to cumulate his votes by giving one candidate as many votes as the number of such Directors multiplied by the number of his shares equal, or by distributing such votes on the same principle among any number of candidates (pursuant to _____).

ARTICLE III. BOARD OF DIRECTORS

SECTION 1. GENERAL POWERS. The business and affairs of the corporation shall be managed by its Board of Directors (pursuant to _____).

SECTION 2. NUMBER, TENURE AND QUALIFICATIONS. The number of Directors of the corporation shall be _____. Each Director shall hold office until the next annual meeting of shareholders and until his successor shall have been elected and qualified (pursuant to _____).

SECTION 3. REGULAR MEETING. A regular meeting of the Board of Directors shall be held without other notice than this Bylaw immediately after, and at the same place as, the annual meeting of shareholders. The Board of Directors may provide, by resolution, the time and place for the holding of additional regular meetings without other notice than such resolution (pursuant to _____).

SECTION 4. SPECIAL MEETINGS. Special meetings of the Board of Directors may be called by or at the request of the President or any two directors. The person or persons authorized to call special meetings of the Board of Directors may fix the place for the holding of any special meeting of the Board of Directors called by them (pursuant to _____).

SECTION 5. NOTICE. Notice of any special meeting shall be given at least three days previously thereto by written notice delivered personally or _____

_____.

SECTION 6. QUORUM. A majority of the number of directors is two and shall constitute a quorum for the transaction of business at any meeting of the Board of Directors (pursuant to _____).

SECTION 7. MANNER OF ACTING. The act of the majority of the directors present at a meeting at which a quorum is present shall be the act of the Board of Directors.

SECTION 8. ACTION WITHOUT A MEETING. Any action that may be taken by the Board of Directors at a meeting may be taken without a meeting if a consent in writing, setting forth the action so to be taken, shall be signed before such action by all of the directors (pursuant to _____).

SECTION 9. VACANCIES. Any vacancy occurring on the Board of Directors may be filled by the affirmative vote of a majority of the remaining directors, though less than a quorum of the Board of Directors, unless otherwise provided by law. A director elected to fill a vacancy shall be elected for the unexpired term of his predecessor in office. Any directorship to be filled by reason of an increase in the number of directors may be filled by election by the Board of Directors for a term of office continuing only until the next election of Directors by the shareholders (pursuant to _____).

ARTICLE IV. OFFICERS

SECTION 1. NUMBER. The officers of the corporation shall be _____. A President, Vice President, Secretary and Treasurer, each of whom shall be elected by the Board of Directors. Such other officers and assistant officers as may be deemed necessary may be elected or appointed by the Board of Directors from time to time (pursuant to _____).

SECTION 2. ELECTION AND TERM OF OFFICE. The officers of the corporation shall be elected annually by the Board of Directors and such election shall be held after each annual meeting of the shareholders. If the election of officers shall not be held at the meetings of the Board of Directors annually, such election shall be held as soon thereafter as conveniently possible. Each officer shall hold office until his successor shall have been duly elected and shall have qualified, or until his death or until he shall resign or shall have been removed in the manner hereinafter provided (pursuant to _____).

SECTION 3. REMOVAL. Any officer or agent may be removed by the Board of Directors whenever, in its judgment, the best interests of the corporation will be served thereby, but such removal shall be without prejudice to the contract rights, if any, of the person so removed. Election or appointment of an officer or agent shall not of itself create contract rights (pursuant to _____).

SECTION 4. VACANCIES. A vacancy in any office because of death, resignation, removal, disqualification or otherwise, may be filled by the Board of Directors for the unexpired portion of the term (pursuant to _____).

SECTION 5. PRESIDENT. The President shall be the principal executive officer of the corporation and, subject to the control of the Board of Directors, shall supervise and control all of the business and affairs of the corporation. He shall, when present, preside at all meetings of the shareholders and of the Board of Directors. He may sign, with the Secretary or any other proper officer of the corporation thereunto authorized by the Board of Directors, certificates for shares of the corporation, any deeds, mortgages, bonds, contracts or other instruments which the Board of Directors has authorized to be executed. He may not sign in cases where the signing and execution thereof shall be expressly delegated by the Board of Directors or by these Bylaws to some other officer or agent of the corporation, or shall be required by law to be otherwise signed or executed; and, in general, the President shall perform all duties incident to the office of President and such of the duties as may be prescribed by the Board of Directors from time to time.

SECTION 6. VICE PRESIDENT. In the absence of the President or in event of his death, inability or refusal to act, the Vice President shall perform the duties of the President and, when so acting, shall have all the powers of and be subject to all the restrictions upon the President. The Vice President shall perform such other duties as from time to time may be assigned to him by the President or by the Board of Directors.

SECTION 7. SECRETARY. The Secretary shall: (a) keep the minutes of the proceedings of the shareholders and of the Board of Directors in one or more books provided for that purpose; (b) see that all notices are duly given in accordance with the provisions of these Bylaws or as required by law; (c) be custodian of the corporate records of the corporation; (d) keep a register of the post office address of each shareholder which shall be furnished to the Secretary by such shareholder; (e) sign with the President, certificates for shares of the corporation, the issuance of which shall have been authorized by resolution of the Board of Directors; (f) have general charge of the stock transfer books of the corporation; (g) in general, perform all duties incident to the office of Secretary and such other duties as from time to time may be assigned to him by the President or by the Board of Directors.

SECTION 8. **TREASURER.** The Treasurer shall (a) have charge and custody of, and be responsible for, all funds and securities of the corporation; (b) receive and give receipts for monies due and payable to the corporation from any source whatsoever, and deposit all such monies in the name of the corporation in such banks, trust companies or other depositories as shall be selected; and (c) in general, perform all of the duties incident to the officer of Treasurer and such other duties as from time to time may be assigned to him by the President or by the Board of Directors.

SECTION 9. **SALARIES.** The salaries of the officers shall be fixed from time to time by the Board of Directors and no officer shall be prevented from receiving such salary by reason of the fact that he is also a director of the corporation.

ARTICLE V. CONTRACTS, LOANS, CHECKS AND DEPOSITS

SECTION 1. **CONTRACTS.** The Board of Directors may authorize any officer or officers, agent or agents, to enter into any contract or execute and deliver any instrument in the name of and on behalf of the corporation, and such authority may be general or confined to specific instances.

SECTION 2. **LOANS.** No loans shall be contracted on behalf of the corporation and no evidence of indebtedness shall be issued in its name unless authorized by a resolution of the Board of Directors. Such authority may be general or confined to specific instances.

SECTION 3. **CHECKS, DRAFTS, ETC.** All checks, drafts or other orders for the payment of money, notes or other evidences of indebtedness issued in the name of the corporation, shall be signed by such officer or officers, agent or agents of the corporation and in such manner as shall from time to time be determined by resolution of the Board of Directors.

SECTION 4. **DEPOSITS.** All funds of the corporation not otherwise employed shall be deposited from time to time to the credit of the corporation in such banks, trust companies or other depositories as the Board of Directors may select.

ARTICLE VI. CERTIFICATES FOR SHARES AND THEIR TRANSFER

SECTION 1. **CERTIFICATES FOR SHARES.** Certificates representing shares of the corporation shall be in such form as shall be determined by the Board of Directors.

Such certificates shall be signed by the President and by the Secretary. All certificates for shares shall be consecutively numbered or otherwise identified. The name and address of the person to whom the shares represented thereby are issued, with the number of shares and date of issue, shall be entered in the stock transfer books of the corporation. All certificates surrendered to the corporation for transfer shall be canceled and no new certificate shall be issued until the former certificate for a like number of shares shall have been surrendered and canceled. In case of a lost, destroyed or mutilated certificate, a new one may be issued upon such terms and indemnity to the corporation as the Board of Directors may prescribe (pursuant to _____).

SECTION 2. <u>TRANSFER OF SHARES.</u> Transfer of shares of the corporation shall be made only on the stock transfer books of the corporation by the holder of record thereof or by his legal representative, who shall furnish proper evidence of authority to transfer, or by his attorney thereunto authorized by Power of Attorney duly executed and filed with the Secretary of the corporation, and on surrender for cancellation of the certificate for such shares. The person in whose name the shares stand on the books of the corporation shall be deemed by the corporation to be the owner thereof for all purposes. Any such transfers may be governed by _____.

ARTICLE VII. AMENDMENTS

These Bylaws may be altered, amended or repealed, and new Bylaws may be adopted by the Board of Directors at any regular or special meeting of the Board of Directors.

ARTICLE VIII. RATIFICATION OF ACTS

The directors and officers of this corporation shall not be personally liable to the corporation or its stockholders for monetary damages for breach of fiduciary duty as a director, except for liability to the extent provided by applicable law (i) for any breach of the director's duty of loyalty to the corporation or its stockholders, (ii) for acts or omissions not in good faith or which involve intentional misconduct or knowing violation of the law, (iii) for any transaction from which the director derived an improper personal benefit, or (iv) under state law. No amendment to or repeal of this Article shall apply to or have any effect on the liability or alleged liability of any director of the corporation for or with respect to any acts or omissions of such director occurring prior to such amendment or repeal. The directors of this corporation have agreed to serve as directors in reliance upon the provisions of this Article.

Form Three

_____ CHECKLIST
FEDERAL ID #_____
(Date Notation of Various Filing)

	1996	1997	1998

Federal Income Tax Return

Secretary of State

Annual Report

State Income Tax Return

Annual Meeting

Dividend

This is not a substitute for legal advice. An attorney must be consulted.

Copyright © 1996 LAW ✔ ™

Form Four

APPLICATION FOR EMPLOYER IDENTIFICATION NUMBER

To be filed with Internal Revenue Service

1. Name (true name as distinguished from trade name)

_____

2. Trade Name, if any (Name under which business is operated, if different from item 1).

_____

3. Social Security Number, if sole proprietor

_____

4. Address of principal place of business (Number and Street)

_____

City and State   Zip

5. Ending month of accounting year

_____

6. County of Business Location

_____

7. Type of organization   __ Individual   __ Trust   __ Partnership
   __ Other   __ Governmental   __ Nonprofit   __ Corporation

8. Date you acquired or started this business (Mo., day, year)

_____

9. Reason for Applying
   __ Started New Business   __ Purchased Going Business   __ Other

10. First date you paid or will pay wages for this business (Mo., day, year)

11. Nature of Business

_____

12. Do you operate more than one place of business?

___ Yes   ___ No

_____

13. Peak number of employees expected in next 12 months (If none, enter "0")

____ Nonagricultural   ____ Agricultural   ____ Household

_____

14. If nature of business is manufacturing, state principal product and raw material used.

_____

15. To whom do you sell most of your products or services?

____ Business establishments   ____ General Public   ____ Other

_____

16. Have you ever applied for an identification number for this or any other business?

____ Yes   ____ No

If yes, enter name and trade name. Also enter approx. date, city, state where you applied and previous number if known.

_____

Date: Signature and Title: Telephone:

_____

Form Five

PRELIMINARY MEETING
OF _____

On the _____ day of _____, 19___, a Preliminary Meeting of the Incorporators of a new _____ Corporation to be known as the _____ Corporation was held at _____ in _____, _____. _____, (legal counsel), was present. _____, _____, _____ were present and will serve as incorporators and as members of the original Board of Directors, along with _____, _____ who were not present.

PURPOSE: At the outset of the meeting, the general discussion related to the purpose of the new corporation which involved the full range of corporate business with particular emphasis on _____ which will be located at _____, _____. The corporate existence begins subsequent to the filing of a Certificate of Incorporation with the Secretary of State.

REGISTERED OFFICE-AGENT-DIRECTORS: It was determined that _____ will serve as the Registered Agent for the corporation and would use his business address at _____, _____ as the registered office of the corporation. In regard to the foregoing, the following resolution passed unanimously:

RESOLVED: That the new Corporation will be known as the _____ (corporation); _____(name) will serve as the Registered Agent for the corporation; the Registered Office for the corporation will be at _____ (location), _____; the original incorporators will serve as the Board of Directors; and an appropriate set of Bylaws will govern the activities of the corporation. The registered office and registered agent are represented to the Secretary of State in conjunction with _____.

BOARD MEMBERS: After the foregoing resolution passed, there was a general discussion relative to the service of Board Members and the individuals incorporating the new business. It was decided that from time to time the members of the Board of Directors would function as officials acting on behalf of the corporation and, in such capacity, the actions of the board should be the sanctioned actions of the company.

RESOLVED: All acts undertaken on behalf of the corporation by the Board of Directors shall be and are hereby ratified as the official acts of the company in order to expedite the organization process.

CAPITALIZATION: The foregoing resolution passed unanimously whereupon the total stock issue and the need for capitalization was reviewed. It was determined that approximately Dollar Amount_____ ($_____) will be needed to start the project.

NO PAR: It was suggested that the total number of shares to be issued by the corporation be at least _____ shares. Some discussion related to the value of the stock and its likelihood to appreciate or depreciate over the years. Therefore, it was suggested that the stock be issued at _____. In this regard the following resolution was proposed.

RESOLVED: That the corporation be authorized to issue an aggregate of _____ shares at _____.

The foregoing resolution passed unanimously whereupon the next order of business was a discussion regarding the interest of various individuals in acquiring stock in the corporation. In this regard _____(names of shareholder) would likely invest Dollar Amount_____ ($_____) each in property interest now held. _____(name of shareholder) discussed the likelihood of investing Dollar Amount_____ ($_____). It was anticipated that each of the individuals would share in the investment made. _____(name of shareholder) indicated an interest in investing Dollar Amount _____ ($_____). At an appropriate time during the next organizational meeting and/or the First Meeting of Directors a resolution would be passed for the issuance of stock in the corporation.

SMALL BUSINESS CORPORATION: It was determined that the corporation would function as a small business corporation with no more than _____ (number) shareholders with a single class of stock and with only individuals, estate and certain trusts eligible as shareholders. Nonresident aliens could not be shareholders.

UNAUTHORIZED ACTS: It is understood that any action taken by the individuals on behalf of the corporation as incorporators are unofficial acts and will remain unofficial acts until the Articles of Incorporation have been filed by the Secretary of State after which a formal Organizational Meeting will be held.

There being no further business, the meeting was declared adjourned.

Dated at _____ on this _____ day of _____, 19___.

_____
ACTING SECRETARY

_____
ACTING PRESIDENT

This is not a substitute for legal advice. An attorney must be consulted.

Form Six

ORGANIZATIONAL MEETING
OF _____

The organizational meeting of _____was called to order on the _____ day of_____, 19___ at _____. Present for the meeting were _____, _____, and _____, all of whom waived formal notice of the meeting. Also present for the meeting was Attorney_____. The first order of business was the discussion by the parties relative to the various documents prepared by counsel.

ARTICLES OF INCORPORATION:

The Articles of Incorporation for the new company were reviewed and discussed. The Articles were accepted by the Secretary of State as filed.

BYLAWS:

The Bylaws drafted on behalf of the corporation, reflecting ___ officers with various duties each, were reviewed by the parties. The Bylaws were approved as read pursuant to the following resolution:

RESOLVED: That the Bylaws drafted for the officers of _____ are hereby adopted as presented.

The foregoing resolution passed unanimously, whereupon the next order of business was a discussion regarding a previous meeting held on the _____ day of _____, 19___, and a review of said meeting minutes from said meeting.

MEETING MINUTES:

The minutes of the meeting held on the _____ day of _____, 19___ were reviewed by the parties present and unanimously approved as official acts of the corporation.

TREASURER'S REPORT:

To date, no treasury had been established, therefore, it was unnecessary for a Treasurer's report to be made.

BANK ACCOUNT:

It was reported by _____ that a bank account would be opened at _____, and the appropriate corporate resolution had been presented for review and adoption by the incorporators.

CAPITALIZATION:

It was decided that the corporation would be capitalized for the sum of $_____ or an investment of $_____ from _____, $_____ from _____ and $_____ from _____. With _____ aggregate shares of the corporation, it was determined that _____ would be initially issued in the amount of $_____ per share. Therefore, a commitment for _____ shares by _____, a commitment for _____ shares by _____ and a commitment for _____ shares by _____ had been made to the corporation. Since cash would be contributed, full compliance was expected with Section 351 of the Internal Revenue Code and, accordingly, the following resolution was adopted:

RESOLVED: That the Board of Directors is authorized to issue a single class of stock in _____ to each shareholder in the amount of $_____ per share in such amounts in proportion as will be agreed by the Board of Directors and the individual shareholders and, in this case, to be up to _____ shares which the Board of Directors will accept in full or in part payment thereof, good and sufficient consideration necessary for the business of the corporation all in compliance to Section 351 of the Internal Revenue Code.

The foregoing resolution was passed unanimously, whereupon each of the parties present, namely_____, _____ and _____ agree to purchase the shares authorized in the following portions:

_____ by _____
_____ by _____
_____ by _____

A single certificate of stock will be issued in the name of each shareholder. It was also determined that in consideration of the stock, would be payment in compliance to Section 351 of the Internal Revenue Code.

SMALL BUSINESS CORPORATION:

It was also determined that _____ would qualify as a small business corporation. It was the intention to keep the corporation in the range of qualification for the benefits allowed by the Internal Revenue Code, and including the possible election of Subchapter S status. In regard to that intention of keeping the corporation a small business entity and in conjunction with the foregoing, the following resolution passed unanimously.

RESOLVED: That _____, being a duly organized corporation under the laws of the State of _____ would be authorized to function as a small business corporation. The initial issue of _____ shares of stock would apply pursuant to the following:

a) Of the initial _____ shares, each share shall be issued at the rate of $ _____ per share;

b) That the initial issue, of no more than _____ shares shall be made for the aggregate capitalization or investment of $_____;

c) The initial issue shall be available to all shareholders or prospective shareholders for the purchase of stock in conjunction with the foregoing up to and including the _____ day of _____, 19___.

d) Only one class of stock shall be issued.

e) The shareholders shall be individuals, estates or certain trusts as permitted by law.

After the foregoing resolution passed unanimously, the form of stock certificate was reviewed by the parties.

STOCK CERTIFICATE:

A review of the proposed stock certificate was made by all parties which unanimously agreed that the stock certificate presented would be the one used by the corporation. The stock certificates shall be in conformity with _____.

SUBCHAPTER S STATUS:

The parties reviewed the 941 form for the purpose of Subchapter S election. It was determined that the parties would elect Subchapter S status and intended to sign the election as soon as the articles were received from the Secretary of State.

RATIFICATION OF ACTS:

It was discussed that all action taken on behalf of _____ be reviewed and approved at each meeting by the Board of Directors or, in this case, the shareholders. Such actions undertaken to date by the corporation were so reviewed, and it was determined that all were properly within the scope and best interest of the corporation and should be ratified accordingly. Therefore, the following resolution was adopted.

RESOLVED: That all actions heretofore taken on behalf of the corporation by the officers, _____, _____, and _____ are hereby ratified as the official acts of the corporation.

ELECTION OF BOARD OF DIRECTORS:

At this point, it was determined that an election of Board of Directors would be held. _____ proposed that the incorporators, namely, _____, _____, and _____, all be elected as the initial Board of Directors. There being no further nominations made, the Board of Directors was unanimously elected as _____, _____, and _____.

ELECTION OF OFFICERS:

After the election of the Board of Directors, a slate of individuals for the officers of the corporation pursuant to the corporate Bylaws was presented. In this regard, the following individuals were elected officers:

_____   _____   _____

PRESIDENT   **VICE PRESIDENT**   **SECRETARY/TREASURER**

Dated at _____ on this _____ day of _____, 19___.

_____

ACTING SECRETARY

This is not a substitute for legal advice. An attorney must be consulted.

Form Seven

OFFICIAL NOTICE
ANNUAL STOCKHOLDERS' MEETING

In accordance with Article II, Section 4 of the Bylaws of _____, as amended, notice is hereby given to stockholders of record of the Annual Meeting of Stockholders at the following time and place:

DATE: _____

TIME: _____

LOCATION: _____

I certify this to be the official notification of the Annual Meeting of Stockholders of _____, and this notice was delivered in accordance with the Bylaws.

_____   _____
President/Secretary   Date

Form Eight

MEETING WAIVER

The undersigned hereby states that notice of a meeting of the Board of Directors of _____ was provided to me on the _____ day of _____, 19___, for a meeting which was to occur on the _____ day of _____, 19___, and I hereby waive formal notice of said meeting and hereby authorize the corporation's Board of Directors to act on my behalf in my absence.

STATE OF _____
COUNTY OF_____

_____
SHAREHOLDER

Subscribed and sworn to before a Notary Public on this _____ day of _____, 19___.

_____
NOTARY PUBLIC, STATE OF _____

This is not a substitute for legal advice. An attorney must be consulted.

Form Nine

FIRST BOARD OF DIRECTORS' MEETING
OF _____
(Name of Corporation)

The first meeting of the Board of Directors of _____ (corporation) was called to order at _____(location) on the _____ day of _____, 19___. Present for the meeting were _____, _____, _____, each of whom waived formal notice of said meeting.

MEETING MINUTES:

The meeting minutes of the Preliminary Meeting held on the _____ day of _____ _____, 19___, and the meeting minutes of the Organizational Meeting on the _____ day of _____, 19___ were read and approved with changes.

TREASURER'S REPORT:

The Treasurer's report was deferred until the next meeting due to the fact that arrangements were being made to open appropriate bank accounts and assemble the funds for the investment by the respective shareholders.

OFFICIAL BUSINESS:

It was anticipated that the first corporate account would be developed sometime within the next 30 days; an appropriate contract would be prepared and signed at that time.

STOCK ISSUE:

It was determined that _____ would qualify as a small business corporation and it was the intention to keep the corporation in the range of qualification for benefits allowed under the Internal Revenue Code including being the election of Sub-chapter S which was decided to be undertaken in the meeting of the general shareholders held on the _____ day of _____, 19___. In regard with the intent of keeping the corporation a small business entity and in conjunction with the foregoing, the following resolution passed unanimously:

RESOLVED: That _____, being a duly organized corporation under the laws of the State of _____, should be authorized to function as a small business corporation and the initial issue of _____ shares of stock would apply pursuant to the following:

A. Of the initial _____ shares, each share shall be issued at the rate of $_____ per share.

B. That, in the initial issue, no more than _____ shares shall be authorized for an aggregate capitalization or investment of $_____.

C. The initial issue shall be available to all shareholders or prospective shareholders for the purchase of stock in conjunction with the foregoing, up to and including the_____ day of_____, 19___.

D. Only a single class of stock shall be issued.

E. The shareholders shall be individuals, estates and/or certain trusts as permitted by law.

After the foregoing resolution passed unanimously, it was decided that the stock certificates would be issued, however, would be held until each investor had invested his complete amount of interest.

FEDERAL I.D. NUMBER:

It was necessary for the corporation to complete its Federal I.D. Application (Form No. 2553), which was completed for filing.

SUBCHAPTER S STATUS:

It was decided that the corporation engage as a Subchapter S; therefore, a Form No. 941 would be completed by the shareholders. All parties agreed that this was the best course for the corporation to follow.

ELECTION OF OFFICERS:

A slate of officers was proposed, and the following individuals were elected as officers of the corporation:

_____President

_____Vice President

_____Secretary

_____Treasurer

NEW BUSINESS:

No new business was discussed at this time.

AMENDMENTS:

No amendments were found to be necessary to the corporation Bylaws.

RATIFICATION OF ACTS:

In conjunction with the parties of the corporation and pursuant to each of the incorporators and officers acting on behalf of the corporation, the following resolution was adopted:

RESOLVED: That all actions heretofore undertaken by each of the officers on behalf of the corporation are hereby authorized as full and complete acts of the corporation; and that the corporation shall indemnify each of the principals, incorporators and shareholders as well as officers for said acts.

The foregoing resolution was passed unanimously. There being no further business, the meeting was declared adjourned.

Dated at _____ on this _____ day of _____, 19___.

_____
SECRETARY

Form Ten

PROXY

I, _____, being a shareholder of _____, do hereby acknowledge receipt of the following items to be discussed at the company annual meeting on _____, 19___:

     1. Notice of the Annual Meeting;

     2. The stated special purpose of the meeting contained in the notice;

     3. A slate of proposed officers;

     4. This Proxy.

In conjunction with the accepted business practices which govern annual meetings under _____ law, I state that I understand the stated purpose of the annual meeting as set forth in the enclosed notice and do hereby provide to _____, President of the _____, my proxy to vote my _____ shares as he deems fit and necessary so long as such vote relates to the enclosed documents.

                                                      _____

                                                  Shareholder's name

Subscribed and sworn to before the undersigned Notary Public of _____ County of the State of _____.

                                    _____

                                    NOTARY PUBLIC, STATE OF _____

Form Eleven

REGISTERED AGENT'S STATEMENT OF RESIGNATION
TO THE _____
FOR THE STATE OF_____:

Pursuant to _____, the undersigned registered agent states:

1. The name of the registered agent is _____.

2. The registered agent resigns the appointment as registered agent for the following corporation:_____.

3. [optional] Upon the effective date of the resignation, the registered office is also discontinued.

The effective date and time of this document is:

_____ [date]

_____ [time]

_____
NAME OF REGISTERED AGENT

_____
[signature]
REGISTERED AGENT

Subscribed and sworn to before a Notary Public on the _____ day of_____, 19___.

_____
NOTARY PUBLIC

This is not a substitute for legal advice. An attorney must be consulted.

Form Twelve

STOCK CERTIFICATE

NUMBER   SHARES

_____   _____

(NAME OF COMPANY)_____

(ADDRESS)_____

THIS CERTIFIES THAT _____ is the owner

of _____ shares of _____ each of the Capital Stock of

_____ transferable only on the books of the Corporation by the holder hereof

in person or by Attorney upon surrender of this Certificate properly endorsed. This Corpo-

ration is organized under the Laws of the State of _____ and pursuant to

the _____.

IN WITNESS WHEREOF, the said Corporation has caused this Certificate to be

signed by its duly authorized officers and to be sealed with the Seal of the Corporation this

_____ day of _____, A.D. 19___.

SHARES _____ EACH

_____   _____

SECRETARY OF CORPORATION   PRESIDENT OF CORPORATION

This is not a substitute for legal advice. An attorney must be consulted.

Copyright © 1996 LAW ✓™

Form Thirteen

AGREEMENT TO RESTRICT TRANSFER OF STOCK

_____
(NAME OF COMPANY)

AGREEMENT made this _____ day of _____, 19____, among _____ (hereinafter "Corporation"), an _____ Corporation with its principal office at _____ and the following individuals (collectively referred to as "stockholders"):

_____

_____

_____

_____

Whereas, the stockholders are the holders of record and beneficial owners of all shares of the issued and outstanding stock of the only issued class of stock of _____ ("Corporation"), an _____ Corporation with its principal office at _____ and;

Whereas, Corporation is an "S" Corporation as defined in Section 1361(a)(1) of the Internal Revenue Code of 1986, having filed an election to be an "S" Corporation on the _____ day of _____, 19___, which was effective as of the first day of its taxable year that began _____ ,19___.

Whereas, the parties desire to continue Corporation "S" election in effect until such time, if any, as the selection is terminated by revocation by Corporation with the consent of the majority of the shares of Corporation's issued and outstanding stock.

Whereas, it is the desire of the parties to restrict the transfer of stock.

Now, therefore, the parties agree as follows:

1. **TERM OF THE AGREEMENT:** The term of this agreement shall be from and including the _____ day of_____, 19___, through and including the day before the first day that Corporation is no longer an "S" Corporation.

2. **DEFINITION OF TRANSFER:** As used in this agreement, the term "transfer" means any sale, exchange, gift, bequest, or any other beneficial ownership of shares of Corporation's stock including, without limitation, a transaction that creates any form of joint ownership in the stock between transferor and one or more persons (whether or not that other person is the spouse of the transferor).

3. **PERMITTED INTERVIVOS TRANSFERS WITHOUT CONSENT OF OTHER SHAREHOLDERS:** The following transfers of stock may be made by a stockholder during his lifetime without the consent of all or any of the other stockholders of the Corporation.

a. **Transfer to Spouse or Children of Stockholder with No Net Increase in the Number of Corporation's Stockholders:** A stockholder may transfer any or all of his shares to his spouse or any one of his children provided that immediately after the transfer, the number of Corporation's stockholders is unchanged from prior to the transfer, as counted by the applicable provisions of the Internal Revenue Code, and the transferee meets all requirements to qualify as an "S" Corporation stockholder.

b. **Transfer to Voting Trust:** A stockholder may transfer all or any part of his shares of stock in a Corporation to a voting trust provided that after the transfer, that stockholder remains the beneficial owner of all of the transferred shares.

c. **Transfers to Grantor Trust:** A stockholder may transfer all or any part of his shares of stock in Corporation to a trust ("grantor trust") provided the following conditions are met:

(i) At all times from the date shares of Corporation's stock are first transferred to the grantor trust through the earlier of the date of the grantor's death or the termination of the trust, the grantor must be treated under the provisions of Subpart E of Part I of Subchapter 1 of Subtitle A of the Internal Revenue Code as in effect on the date of the transfer, as the owner of the trust.

(ii) If the grantor trust is to continue for the grantor's life, then on the death of the grantor, the trust must terminate and all shares of Corporation's stock held by the trust must be distributed in accordance with Paragraph 6.

(iii) If the grantor trust can terminate before the death of the grantor, the trust agreement must provide that on the termination of the trust, all shares of Corporation's stock must be distributed to the grantor.

4. **TRANSFERS PERMITTED AFTER STOCK IS OFFERED TO CORPORATION OR OTHER SHAREHOLDERS:** A stockholder shall not, during his lifetime, transfer or dispose of any portion or all of his stock interest in the Corporation other than as provided for in Paragraph 3, unless he shall first offer in writing such stock to Corporation at a purchase price to be established annually by a majority vote of the Board of Directors. If the stock is not purchased by the Corporation within 90 days of the receipt of the offer, then the stock not so purchased shall be offered for sale at same price and shall be subject to an option on the part of each of the shareholders to purchase, at a minimum, the number of shares proportionate to their current stockholding in the Corporation. The option to

purchase stock by the other shareholders must be exercised within 30 days from the time such option became available to the shareholders. If all of the stock of the stockholder desiring to make a disposition thereof is not purchased by the Corporation or other shareholders within 120 days after same is offered for such sale, the selling stockholder shall have the option of selling or transferring his stock in the Corporation to any other as follows, provided that the stock is not sold or transferred at a price less than was offered to the Corporation or other stockholders:

a. **Transfers of all Shares to United States Citizen:** Any stockholder may transfer all, but not less than all, of his shares to an individual who is a citizen of the United States at the time the transfer is made provided that the transferer retains no interest in those shares (whether as a joint tenant owner, beneficiary, trustee, creditor, or otherwise) after the transfer.

b. **Transfer of Some of Shares to United States Citizen:** Any stockholder may transfer less than all of his shares to an individual who is a citizen of the United States at the time the transfer is made, provided that the majority of Corporation's shareholders approve of the transaction and that, immediately after the transfer, the number of the Corporation's stockholders does not exceed the maximum number an "S" Corporation is allowed to have under the applicable provisions of the Internal Revenue Code, as then in effect.

c. **Transfers to Trust Owned by Individual Other Than Grantor:** A stockholder may transfer all or any part of his shares of stock in the Corporation to a trust ("beneficiary trust") provided that the following conditions are met:

(i) One individual ("beneficiary") who is a citizen of the United States, must be treated under the provisions of Subpart E of Part I of Subchapter J of Chapter 1 of Subtitle A of the Internal Revenue Code as in effect on the date of the transfer, as the owner of all of the trust at all times from the date shares of the Corporation's stock are first transferred to the trust through the earlier of the date of the beneficiary's death or the date of the termination of the trust.

(ii) If less than all of a stockholder's shares of Corporation's stock are transferred to the beneficiary trust, and if the beneficiary is not already a stockholder in the Corporation at the time of the transfer, then provided that the majority of the Corporation's shareholders approve of the transaction and that, immediately after the transfer, the number of the Corporation's stockholders does not exceed the maximum number a Sub-S Corporation is allowed to have under the applicable provisions of the Internal Revenue Code, as then in effect.

(iii) If the beneficiary trust is to continue for the beneficiary's life, the trust agreement must provide that, on the death of the beneficiary, the trust must terminate and all the shares of the Corporation's stock held by the trust must be distributed to one individual who is a citizen of the United States.

(iv) If the beneficiary trust can terminate before the death of the beneficiary, the trust agreement must provide that on the termination of the trust, all shares of the Corporation's stock must be distributed to the beneficiary.

5. **PERMITTED INTERVIVOS TRANSFERS WITH CONSENT OF OTHER STOCKHOLDERS:** A stockholder may make a transfer not described in Paragraph 3 or Paragraph 4 of this agreement of all or any of his shares of stock in the Corporation to any person who, under the applicable provisions of the Internal Revenue Code in effect at the time of the transfer, is eligible to be stockholder in an "S" Corporation, provided all of the following conditions are met:

a. Immediately after the transfer, the number of Corporation's stockholders does not exceed the maximum number an "S" Corporation is allowed to have under the applicable provisions of the Internal Revenue Code, as then in effect.

b. All persons who are stockholders in the Corporation at the time of the transfer must consent in writing to the transfer.

6. **TRANSFER BY WILL OR BY OPERATION OF LAW AT DECEDENT'S DEATH:** Transfer of stock due to the death and/or pursuant to the Last Will and Testament of any shareholders must satisfy the requirement of Paragraphs 3, 4 or 5 of this agreement.

7. **TRANSFERS TO INELIGIBLE PERSONS:** Each stockholder agrees to not transfer, or attempt to transfer, any shares of stock in the Corporation now owned by that stockholder, or hereafter acquired by that stockholder, to a person who is not eligible to be a stockholder of an "S" Corporation under the provisions of the Internal Revenue Code as in effect at the time of the transfer.

8. **TRANSFER OF SHARES IN VIOLATION OF AGREEMENT NULL AND VOID:** Any purported transfer of shares of Corporation's stock made in violation of the provisions of this agreement shall be null and void and the purported transfer shall be declared voidable.

9. **GRANT OF OPTION:** A stockholder may not grant, sell, give or, in any way, create in any person any option, warrant or other right (including any "option" to acquire all or any part of that shareholder's shares of Corporation's stock) if that person is not eligible to be a stockholder in an "S" Corporation at the time of the grant, etc.) A shareholder may not grant, sell, give or, in any way, create in any person who is eligible to be a shareholder

in an "S" Corporation any option to acquire all or any part of that shareholder's shares of Corporation's stock unless the following requirements are met:

a. The option must be in writing.

b. The option must specifically provide that the exercise of the right to acquire stock will be treated as a transfer for purposes of this agreement and that the option may not be exercised if:

(i) The holder, at the time of the proposed exercise, is not eligible to be a shareholder of an "S" Corporation even if the holder was eligible at the time they obtained the option, or;

(ii) Immediately after the exercise of the option, the number of Corporation's stockholders would exceed the maximum number an "S" Corporation is allowed to have under the applicable provisions of the Internal Revenue Code, as then in effect. In the event of change in the Internal Revenue Code, this agreement should be modified to appropriately conform in order to maintain the "S" Corporation status.

c. All persons who are stockholders in the Corporation at the time of the grant, etc. of the option must consent in writing to the grant, etc.

Any purported grant, etc., of an option to a person not eligible to be a stockholder in an "S" Corporation or to an eligible person in violation of any of the above requirements shall be null and void. Any purported exercise of an option purported to be granted whose grant is null and void shall be null and void and shall be ineffective to create any interest in the purported grantee in any shares of Corporation's stock. Any purported exercise of an option validly granted shall be null and void if that exercise would create any interest in shares of Corporation's stock in a person not eligible to be a stockholder in an "S" Corporation.

10. **PLEDGE OF STOCK:** A stockholder may not pledge, hypothecate, or otherwise create a security interest in all or part of that stockholder's shares of stock in the Corporation without first obtaining the consent, in writing, of all persons who are stockholders in the Corporation at the time of the proposed pledge, etc.

11. **ENDORSEMENT ON STOCK CERTIFICATE:** There shall be legibly stamped on each stock certificate issued by the Corporation during the time this agreement is in effect the following statement:

"None of the shares of stock represented by this certificate may be transferred, no interest in all or any of those shares (whether as owner, creditor or otherwise) may be created, and no right to acquire all or any of those shares may be obtained, except in compliance with the terms of the Stock Transfer Agreement dated the _____day of _____, 19___, among _____ (name of company) and its then stockholders. A copy of that agreement is on file in the office of the Secretary of the Corporation. Any interest created in any of the shares represented by this certificate in violation of the terms of that agreement shall be null and void.

12. **TRANSFERS BOUND BY AGREEMENT:** Notwithstanding anything else contained in this agreement, no transfer of shares during the term of this agreement shall be effective to vest any right, title or ownership, in the transferee unless the transferee agrees, in writing, in an instrument filed with the Secretary of the Corporation, to be bound by all the provisions of this agreement. Without limiting the foregoing, a transferee, by accepting any transferred shares, shall be deemed to have become a party to this agreement with respect to those transferred shares to the same extent as if that transferee had executed this agreement.

13. **INDEMNIFICATION FOR BREACH:** If any stockholder breaches any term of this agreement in a manner that causes the Corporation's Subchapter "S" election to terminate, that stockholder ("indemnitor") shall indemnify each of the other stockholders ("indemnitees") for the amount of that stockholder's share of lost Federal Income Tax benefits resulting from the termination during the period the Corporation is ineligible to make a Subchapter "S" election under the applicable provisions of the Internal Revenue Code.

a. Definition of Federal Income Tax Benefits: For purposes of this Paragraph 13, a stockholder's share of Federal Income Tax benefits equals the excess of:

(i) The stockholder's pro rata share of Federal Income Taxes imposed on the Corporation as a "C" Corporation plus the stockholder's Federal Income Tax on dividend distributions by the Corporation, over

(ii) The stockholder's pro rata share of Federal Income Taxes that would have been imposed on the Corporation as an "S" Corporation if it had the same items of income, loss, deduction and credit that has a "C" Corporation, plus the amount of Federal Income Taxes that the stockholder would have paid on the items of income, etc., that would have been passed through to the stockholder if it were an "S" Corporation. The Corporation and the stockholders shall make reasonable efforts to mitigate the loss of Federal Income Tax benefits resulting from the termination by seeking to have the termination treated as inadvertent under Section 1352(f) of the Internal Revenue Code. If the termination is not treated as inadvertent, the Corporation and the stockholders shall seek the Secretary of the Treasury's consent to a new election as soon as possible.

14. **BENEFIT:** This agreement shall be binding upon and shall insure to the benefit of the parties to this agreement, and their respective heirs, executors, administrators, legal representatives, and assignees.

15. **APPLICABLE LAW:** This agreement shall be governed by, and interpreted and construed under and in accordance with, the laws of the State of _____.

16. **MODIFICATION:** No modification, rescission, cancellation, amendment or termination of this agreement shall be effective unless it is in writing and is signed by all parties to the agreement. In the event of change in the Internal Revenue Code, this agreement shall be modified to appropriately conform to preserve its "S" Corporation status.

17. **COUNTERPARTS:** This agreement may be executed in two or more counterparts, each of which shall be deemed an original and all of which, taken together, shall constitute one agreement.

18. **NOTIFICATION OF TRANSFER:** The Corporation must be given written notice not less than 30 days prior to any proposed transfer of stock ownership. Such written notification must include sufficient information to insure that the terms of this agreement will be met by the proposed transfer.

In witness whereof, the parties have executed this agreement:

_____   _____
Name of Shareholder   Signature of Shareholder

_____   _____
Name of Shareholder   Signature of Shareholder

_____   _____
Name of Shareholder   Signature of Shareholder

Approved on behalf of _____ by:

_____   _____
PRESIDENT   **SECRETARY**

Form Fourteen

STOCK REGISTER

Certificate Number	Date of Issue	Shareholder's Name	Address	Shares in Certificate

This is not a substitute for legal advice. An attorney must be consulted.

Copyright © 1996 LAW ™

Index